NEITHER CONSERVATIVE NOR LIBERAL:
The Burger Court on Civil Rights and Liberties

Edited by

Francis Graham Lee
Saint Joseph's University

ROBERT E. KRIEGER PUBLISHING COMPANY
MALABAR, FLORIDA
1983

Original Edition 1983

Printed and Published by
ROBERT E. KRIEGER PUBLISHING COMPANY. INC.
KRIEGER DRIVE
MALABAR, FL 32950

Copyright © 1983 by
ROBERT E. KRIEGER PUBLISHING COMPANY, INC.

All rights reserved. No part of this book may be reproduced in any form or by any electronic or mechanical means including information storage and retrieval systems without permission in writing from the publisher.

Printed in the United States of America.

Library of Congress Cataloging in Publication Data

Lee, Francis Graham.
   Neither conservative nor liberal.

   Bibliography: p.
   Includes index.
   1. Civil rights—United States. 2. United States. Supreme Court. 3. Burger, Warren E., 1907-   . I. Title.
KF4749.L37   342.73'085'02643   82-120
ISBN 0-89874-425-3   347.3028502643   AACR2

To

Celine

Francis Graham Lee is Associate Professor of Politics at Saint Joseph's University. Articles by Dr. Lee have appeared recently in the *International Review of History and Political Science, State and Local Government Review,* and *America.*

Contents

INTRODUCTION

"War," wrote Georges Clemenceau, "is too important to be left to generals." For a growing number of Americans, constitutional law seems too important to be left solely to judges, even if they are the justices of the United States Supreme Court. Twice in the past twelve years—in 1968 and again in 1980—Supreme Court decisions have become major issues in presidential campaigns. Even when they have not been at the center of the political stage, constitutional issues have continued to make their presence felt as in 1972 when the infamous Committee to Re-Elect the President sought to link the candidacy of George McGovern in the public's mind with the three A's of acid, amnesty, and abortion and in 1976 when both candidates Ford and Carter took the Court to task for the *Miranda* rule requiring police to warn suspects of their constiutional rights before beginning any questioning.

Of course, making a political issue out of the Court is hardly a new tactic. Jefferson, Lincoln, and Franklin Roosevelt all sought political advantage attacking the judiciary. More recently, in the 1950s, both Southern segregationists and professional anti-Communists played up to their political galleries by introducing impeachment resolutions aimed at the judges they held responsible for either outlawing segregated schools (*Brown v. Board of Education*, 1954) or crippling the Smith Act's ability to control the American Communist Party (*Yates v. United States*, 1957). The posturings of a Strom Thurmond, a John Marshall Butler, or a Robert Welch, however, are light-years away from the rhetoric of Richard Nixon in 1968 or of Ronald Reagan and the Republican Party Platform of 1980. The Southern Manifesto and the Impeach Earl Warren billboards that sprouted along the nation's highways in the late fifties and early sixties were generally seen as well outside the political mainstream, as somehow illegitimate. Thus, although Dwight Eisenhower's recently discovered misgivings about the Court's entering the school segregation dispute were probably not unlike those of many north of the Mason-Dixon Line, "massive resistance" won scant support or sympathy outside the South. Whether one liked what the Court had said and done in *Brown* or not was not important. What was important was that the Court had spoken and while this might not mean that you would applaud the Court, it did mean that you would not actively oppose it. The same was true of the decisions that triggered the Jenner-Butler Bill of 1958. Court endorsement of First Amendment rights for members of the American Communist Party, handed down on what was to be called, "Red Monday," was hardly popular, but restricting the right of the Supreme Court to hear such cases seemed to other than the most bitter court critics even more un-American.

Today, only those who agree with the results achieved by the Court's decisions are likely to be terribly disturbed with Senator Jesse Helms's (Rep.–N.C.) effort at limiting the Court's appellate jurisdiction in cases involving prayer in the public schools or the efforts of the same North Carolinian and his allies to reverse the Court's decisions allowing abortion. A committee set up during the 1980 campaign to rally opposition to a Republican Party platform pledging that party to support the appointment of federal judges who champion what the GOP decided were family values—in other words, single issue judges—made little real impression except to rally those who felt personally threatened by the Republican Party's policy positions on these "family issues."

All of this represents a change for the Court and its role in the American political system, a change that is perhaps as significant as anything that has occurred since the famous "switch in time that saved nine" of 1937, when the Court abandoned its traditional role as defender of property rights and assumed a new role as guardian of civil rights and liberties.

The significance of this development can probably best be understood by borrowing a concept, scope of conflict, first introduced by E.E. Schattschneider in his book, *The Semi-Sovereign People*. For Schattschneider all political action can be seen as revolving around efforts directed at either expanding or contracting the scope of conflict, in other words, at attempts to increase or decrease the number of people involved in a political issue. Groups or individuals who are in agreement with the *status quo* generally will seek to maintain the existing scope of conflict, confident that they will be able to maintain their dominance in that forum. Those who disagree will frequently attempt to alter the scope of conflict, either by bringing new combatants into the conflict, people they hope will side with them, or by seeking to exclude those current participants who oppose their position.

Schattschneider offers a very graphic example of this process in a story of how a race riot occurred in Chicago during the Second World War. It appears to have started simply enough with a fistfight involving two individuals. Race appears not even to have been a factor. Somehow, the spectators got into the fray, then the neighborhood and finally a large section of the city found itself embroiled. The scope so expanded that the original dispute was lost sight of and the original disputants forgotten. Of course, most fistfights don't evolve into citywide riots. Most are probably ended when one brawler sufficiently pummels the other and proves his superiority, but this is true of most political disputes as well. Until recently, it was surely true of most disputes involving constitutional issues. The scope of conflict and, accordingly, the number of people potentially involved were severely limited. It included the parties to the suit, their lawyers, judges, usually state judges but increasingly federal judges, and, only occasionally, constitutional scholars. Rarely, however, were members of Congress involved and hardly ever did such a controversy catch the public's attention.

That Congress and the public were not involved was scarcely accidental. Their participation was widely accepted as violating the prevailing norms of the then dominant political culture. When F.D.R., for example, made the Court a political issue in 1936, he clearly was trying to expand the scope of conflict. In the existing arena, the Supreme Court, he could not win as he had learned in *Schechter, Carter* and *Panama Refining v. Ryan*; the conservatives simply had more votes among "the nine old men." Only by seeking to involve the people and the Congress, by expanding the scope of conflict, could he hope to win; but making a political issue of the Court was easier said than done. Public opinion still viewed the Court as somehow sacrosanct. They had yet to accept Max Lerner's dictum about judicial decisions not being brought by constitutional storks. The same problem served to becalm Court critics in the fifties. In both instances, efforts to expand the scope of conflict failed because people saw such a move as politically illegitimate. Constitutional disputes were to be left to the judges. They were not political and so neither politicians nor the public had a proper role in such controversies.

American attitudes are quite different today. Where Roosevelt failed, Nixon was to succeed in 1968 with his appeals for a Court committed to strengthening "the peace forces" in American society. By and large, Americans had finally accepted the notion that unpopular Court decisions could be reversed not simply by appeals to constitutional principles, but by appeals to "the silent majority."

It had taken a while for Americans to come to this conclusion. The thirties might have shaken the faith in constitutional storks among avid Court watchers, but it had had little effect upon the mass of Americans. The jurisprudence of the fifties and sixties did. The end of "separate but equal," the advent of "one man, one vote," the Court's proclamation of a radically new code of criminal rights, all these destroyed whatever had survived of the idea of an unchanging Constitution and the corresponding belief that "it is not the judges who speak, but the Constitution that speaks through them."

The democratizing tides of the sixties probably also played a part in these changes. The forces that destroyed the power of party bosses and ended the era in which political nominations could be determined by party professionals did not leave the judiciary untouched. If the people were fit to choose a president, if congressional candidates could be held strictly accountable for each of their votes, it seemed to follow that these same people could not very well be excluded completely from the judicial process.

Just as Johnson and Nixon could not limit debate on the war in Southeast Asia to the National Security Council, but found the debate expanding almost inevitably to include first the campus demonstrators, then the Congress and finally most of the country, so the Court today finds that controversy does not end on decision day. Indeed, the announcement of a decision by the Court may at most serve only to channel further debate.

Still, all of this simply explains why it is possible today to involve a large segment of the population in debates on constitutional questions, why, more specifically, Nixon succeeded in expanding the scope of conflict whereas F.D.R. had failed. The 1968 election easily could have been unique. Instead it appears to have established a pattern, a pattern that seems to have been perpetuated largely as a result of decisions by the very Court created by Richard Nixon.

The Warren Court rulings, the democratization of American political life, the decline of parties, all of these were major factors in creating a climate in which broad conflict over constitutional issues would be perceived as legitimate. These factors, however, by no means guaranteed that such issues would remain on the political agenda throughout the seventies and into the eighties.

By the seventies, for instance, many of the controversies sparked by the Warren Court had pretty much run their course. Opposition to *Brown* had pretty much disappeared. *Baker v. Carr* (1962) and *Reynolds v. Sims* (1964), decisions which had earlier provoked efforts to call a constitutional convention to overturn them, were also largely accepted. Even the criminal rights decisions stirred less controversy as crime rates began to taper off.

The fact that the Court and specific constitutional issues remain at the center of political controversy today is attributable almost entirely to the Burger Court and its decisions.

Busing, abortion and equal rights for women are all the products of a Court that is largely the creation of Richard Nixon, the man who as a presidential candidate in 1968 took the then sitting Court and its members severely to task for allegedly reading into the Constitution their own personal ideas and prejudices and who promised, if elected, that he would appoint only "strict constructionists," judges who would support the "peace forces," judges who would be responsive to the needs and concerns of "the silent majority."

Accordingly, it was a little ironic that the success of the Republican Party in recapturing the White House in 1980 and winning the Senate for the first time since 1954 was the result at least in part of a strategy that hoped that by attacking these decisions and the values they represented to allow the GOP to win votes among traditionally Democratic blocs. It also demonstrated the fascinating whimsy of the political game, for the Republican attacks in 1980, unlike those mounted by Nixon in 1968, were directed at a Court which was overwhelmingly a Republican product. Only Justices White and Marshall of the 1980 Court had been nominated to the bench by Democratic presidents. All the rest were appointed by Republican chief executives: Brennan and Stewart by Eisenhower; Burger, Blackmun, Powell, and Rehnquist by Nixon; and Stevens by Ford—though two, Brennan and Powell, are themselves Democrats.

This is the Burger Court or as it once was more popularly known, the Nixon Court. Rarely has a Court been created as swiftly. In a span of less than three years, Nixon was able to make four appointments, appointments whose actual significance was increased still further by the fact that three of the judges who were replaced had been part of the liberal majority that had dominated the Supreme Court from the time of Justice Felix Frankfurter's retirement in 1962—a majority which at the time of Richard Nixon's election seemed to number six judges: Black, Brennan, Douglas, Fortas, Marshall, and Warren.

Nixon's first opportunity to remake the Court and fulfill his campaign promise came with the retirement of Chief Justice Earl Warren, the man who more than anyone else typified both the positive and negative aspects of the Warren Court, a judge who by his actions showed himself much more concerned with questions of fairness and justice than with points of law, let alone with "neutral principles of constitutional law."

Warren had announced his attention to step aside in 1968, thereby enabling lame-duck President Lyndon Johnson to promote his good friend and sometime advisor, Associate Justice Abe Fortas, to the post of Chief Justice. The choice of Fortas, a highly qualified jurist, must have pleased the outgoing Chief who surely could sense in Fortas someone who would carry on the legacy of the Warren years. Fortas's nomination was not as warmly received in other quarters. In the Senate in particular it provided an opportunity for critics of the Court to go on a rampage. Senator Strom Thurmond (Rep.–S.C.), now a Republican but still a Court critic, greeted the hapless Fortas with shouts of "*Mallory, Mallory,*" ignoring the fact that Fortas had not even been on the bench when the Court had reversed Mallory's rape conviction—freed, Mallory would later be arrested and convicted of murder—because of the failure of federal authorities to take Mallory to a federal magistrate "without unnecessary delay." North Carolina's Sam Erwin (Dem.) was more restrained but equally devastating as he quoted in his upcountry drawl from certain Fortas opinions and speeches that indicated Fortas was not inclined to be bound by either the words of the Constitution or the intent of its framers.

Fortas's nomination also ran into trouble on other fronts. Senate liberals raised questions about the propriety of Fortas's having acted as an adviser to L.B.J. while serving as a justice. Particularly troubling were revelations that Fortas had counselled the President as to how far he could go in suppressing antiwar protest without violating First Amendment rights. The final blow to the nomination, however, came when it was revealed that Fortas had accepted several rather substantial fees for lectures given while a justice. The combination of forces opposed to confirmation was finally too great and faced with the prospect of a filibuster by Republicans and Southern Democrats, Johnson acted to withdraw the nomination from Senate consideration. Following Nixon's election in November of the same year, speculation developed that Johnson would nominate popular former Justice Tom Clark and thus deny his successor the opportunity of choosing a chief justice; but, despite the rumors, no action was taken.

For a while, the Nixon election also raised speculation as to whether the vacancy still existed or whether Warren would reconsider and deprive his old California adversary of an opportunity to select a chief justice. Warren, however, carried through on his promise and stepped down in 1969. To succeed Warren, Nixon nominated Federal Appeals Court Judge Warren Burger, one of the more outspoken judicial critics of the Warren Court.

Further revelations about Fortas's financial dealings led to his unexpected resignation later in 1969, the first instance of a Supreme Court justice being forced to resign because of alleged financial wrongdoing. Nixon chose another Minnesota native, Federal Appeals Judge Harry Blackmun to succeed Fortas. Old acquaintances, Burger and Blackmun were soon dubbed "the Minnesota twins."

The 1971 retirement of Associate Justices Hugo Black and John Marshall Harlan, both of whom were to die shortly afterwards, gave Nixon two additional openings. To fill Black's seat, Nixon nominated a former American Bar Association President, conservative Virgina Democrat Lewis Powell. Assistant Attorney General William Rehnquist, a former law clerk for Justice Robert Jackson and political disciple of Senator Barry Goldwater, was named to the Harlan vacancy.

The Nixon judges together with either Potter Stewart or Byron White, seemed well positioned to end the era of the Warren Court. Both supporters and critics of Nixon's plan for a "strict constructionist" Court agreed that the Court as now remade would surely play a less visible role in American life than had its predecessor. Both were wrong.

As much as the Warren Court, the Burger Court has acted to raise or redefine issues ignored by the other two branches of government. Just as *Brown* and *Baker* had set the tone for much of the domestic political debates of the fifties and sixties by addressing the problems of segregation and legislative malapportionment, *Roe* (abortion), *Swann* (busing), *Frontiero* (sex discrimination), and *Bakke* (racial quotas) have dominated much of the political discussion and debate of the seventies and are likely to continue to do so well into the eighties. In so doing, the Court has found itself enmeshed in at least as much controversy as the Warren Court. In fact, as indicated above, the position in which the Court currently finds itself is potentially more dangerous than anything faced by the Court since the time of the American Civil War. Critics of the Court not only find the judiciary with few allies, but realize that there exists now little resistance to efforts to politicize the Court's decisions and to seek political remedies to judgments with which they disagree.

Yet, while it is clear that the Burger Court has had a significant impact upon our lives and that many of its rulings have been highly controversial, it is not altogether clear exactly what that effect has been and, as a result for those who disagree with it, how it can be countered. The nomination of Sandra Day O'Connor is a good example of this in the divisions it created in the alliance that had supported Reagan in 1980.

Prior to 1937, the role of the Supreme Court, indeed of the entire federal judicial establishment, was to protect the rights of private property. From John Marshall to Charles Evans Hughes, the Court could almost always be depended on to come down on the side of those who opposed government regulation of property. Out of the debacle left by "the switch in time that saved nine," the Stone Court (1941-1946) sought to chart an entirely new course for the Court by emphasizing a concern for individual rights, going so far as to hint at a judicial "double standard" that placed civil liberties well above property rights in terms of judicial concern. The Vinson Court (1946-1953) slowed down this process slightly, seeing it as necessary at least for a time for the Court to join forces with the other two branches of the federal government in order to repel what was perceived as a grave internal threat posed by the American Communist Party.

The Warren Court (1953-1969) returned to the direction first taken by Stone and his brethren and showed during its sixteen years not only a commitment to civil liberties but a desire to reshape all of American society in a more egalitarian mode.

Based on their overall performances, the Hughes (1930-1941) and Vinson Courts have generally been labeled as conservative, the Stone and Warren Courts liberal; but, these terms do not convey the full flavor of these Courts. The conservatism of the Hughes and Vinson Courts was quite different and the difference arose only in part from the fact that the former was largely preoccupied by questions of property rights while the latter's time in the main was absorbed by issues arising from the problems of balancing individual rights with government ability to function and even to survive. Likewise the common liberalism of the Stone and Warren Courts does not even partially bridge the significant gulf that clearly divides them.

The other variable necessary to understand these differences is judicial philosophy or, to put it another way, what role the judges perceive the Court as properly playing within the framework of democratic government in America. The activist philosophy, held by judges as different as Marshall, Taney, and Taft, believes that the Court, as a coequal branch of government, has not only the right but the duty to say what is and what is not constitutional and to oppose any action by President, Congress or the states that runs counter to this interpretation. The competing philosophy is that of judicial self-restraint. As expressed by justices such as Holmes, Cardozo, and Frankfurter, it emphasizes the political weakness of the Court, its undemocratic character and, as a result, urges that the power to declare a law unconstitutional and hence void be used only when another unit of government has clearly violated the Constitution. The Hughes and Warren Courts generally opted for the activist course; the Stone and Vinson Courts, different in so many other ways, tended to follow in the pattern of self-restraint.

Using these two variables, political philosophy and judicial philosophy, students of the Court can construct a simple two by two table that can be used to categorize similarly oriented courts. The system of classification (Figure 1) functions well not only with twentieth century courts, but earlier courts as well. Thus the Taney Court falls fairly easily into the category of activist-conservative; the Waite Court, self-restraint-conservative. Classifying the Burger Court, however, poses a problem.

Judicial Philosophy

		Activist	Self-Restraint
	Conservative	Hughes	Vinson
Political Philosophy			
	Liberal	Warren	Stone

Figure 1.

Is it conservative? Richard Nixon certainly hoped so. "Strict constructionist" was generally regarded as a codeword for conservative. Certainly, "strict constructionist" judges were not expected to be judicial innovators. In the area of criminal rights, this has usually been the case. *Mapp* (1961) and *Miranda* (1966), though not overruled, have been narrowly interpreted thereby allowing government use under certain limited conditions of both illegally obtained evidence and confessions. On the other hand, the Burger Court broke new ground when it found a constitutional barrier to certain types of government regulation of abortion (*Roe v. Wade,* 1972) and to state and federal legislation treating women differently solely because they were women (*Reed v. Reed,* 1971 and *Frontiero v. Richardson,* 1973).

Classifying the Burger Court as inclined to either activism or self-restraint also is difficult to do. *Roe* and *Frontiero* seem clear instances of activism as do

Swann v. Charlotte-Mecklenberg Board of Education (1971) and *Keyes v. School District* (1973). Yet, subsequent decisions allowing government apparently to use its power to discourage abortions (*Harris v. McRae,* 1980), its refusal to label sex a "suspect category," and its maintenance of the distinction between *de facto* and *de jure* segregation, all seem to indicate a certain deference to the wishes of the other two branches of government and to public opinion.

The fact that the Court seems difficult to label has prompted some to say that the Burger Court is perhaps the most politically motivated court in the history of the nation, their position being that the Court is in fact making its decisions based on what it at any given moment perceives to be politically expedient. Others claim the explanation can be found in the lack of leadership provided by Chief Justice Burger. Still, others take the position that it is the overwhelming mediocrity of the current Court that prevents it from adopting any consistent course of action.

Whatever the correct answer, today it has become a matter of concern and interest not only to professional court watchers and those who ply their trade before the federal courts, but to the much larger public who very likely will have much to say about the final impact of such Burger Court decisions as *Roe, Swann,* and *Frontiero.* Their ability effectively to play this newly assigned role, however, depends on their understanding more about the Burger Court, what it is and what it is not, much more than they can get from the overly simplified portrayals of the Court furnished by politicians on the campaign trail or by most of the popular media.

The Burger Court is a terribly complex entity, too complex as Chicago Law Professor Philip Kurland has warned "to paint with a broad brush and in a single color." Neither wholly liberal nor conservative, activist or self-restraintist, it has generated an almost unprecedented outpouring of scholarly comment. This ranges from analyses of its legal craftsmanship, to case studies devoted to its record in handling both the old issues of free speech and religious freedom and the new problems of abortion and sex discrimination.

The selections that follow are intended to give the reader an opportunity to sample some of this scholarship and to gain from it a better understanding of the issues that face the Court today and how the Court has responded to these issues.

Part One
DUE PROCESS AND EQUAL PROTECTION

CHAPTER 1   "From Warren to Burger: The Rise and Decline of Substantive Equal Protection"*

WALLACE MENDELSON**

To judge the political or judicial philosophy of the Burger Court requires more than measuring it against some accepted contemporary norm for liberalism or conservatism, activism or self-restraint. Rather it requires an additional comparison, a comparison of the current Court to its predecessors, most importantly to its immediate predecessor.

Absent such a comparison, it is difficult to make the argument, as many indeed do, that the Burger Court is conservative. The present Court, according to almost any standard of liberalism, rates high. It is conservative only in comparison with the Warren Court and not necessarily with the Warren Court of history, but rather with a Court that never was, the Court that exists only in the minds of those who speculate what the Warren Court would have done, given the same circumstances and opportunities, with the cases that have come before the Burger Court.

Political Scientist Wallace Mendelson gives us some basis for such speculation in the following article which deals with issues arising under the Equal Protection Clause of the Fourteenth Amendment.

*Copyright © 1972, American Political Science Association. Reprinted by permission of the author and the A.P.S.A. from 66 *American Political Science Review* (1972), pp. 1226-1233.
**Professor of Government, University of Texas.

We cannot have equal justice under law except we have some law.

Robert H. Jackson

Substantive due process remains that classic—if temporary—achievement of judicial activism. Its demolition by the Roosevelt Court reflected an unmistakable mandate of the American people. "Equal protection" ran a similar course, reaching its zenith perhaps in the *Sewer Pipe Case*[1] (invalidating an antitrust law because it applied to business, but not to farm, operations), and *Truax v. Corrigan*[2] (invalidating a restriction on antilabor injunctions because it limited protection of some, not all, property). The Roosevelt Court's response to this mangling of the power to govern was revealed in *Kotch*[3] (nepotism is not forbidden in issuing river pilot licenses), *Goesaert*[4] (in granting barmaid licenses a state may favor wives and daughters of male bar owners), and *Lee Optical*[5] (sale of prescription eyeglasses by opticians may be regulated, though sale of ready-made glasses by others is not). Judges who found no unconstitutional discrimination in these cases could hardly be expected to find it in other non-race controversies. The Court's test was lenient:

> State legislatures are presumed to have acted within their constitutional power despite the fact that, in practice, their laws result in some inequality. A statutory discrimination will not be set aside if any state of facts reasonably may be conceived to justify it . . .[6]

Surely many legislators whose votes can be explained only in terms of pressure group realities must have been fascinated with the ingenuity of judges in conceiving grounds that might justify *Kotch*-like classifications. Seared by what had gone before, and confident that freedom to make mistakes is far too important to be left entirely to judges, the Roosevelt Court abandoned substantive equal protection, just as it abandoned substantive due process. Liberals now seem to have forgotten that from Jefferson's day until well into the Warren era liberalism on the bench meant keeping hands off legislation—except increasingly to protect Bill of Rights, or racial, freedoms. The rationale no doubt was that with special court protection for these basic interests, the people are quite capable of governing themselves, and must be permitted to do so. As a matter of statistics only two cases after the Roosevelt Court revolution (1937) until the middle years of the Warren era violated this precept.[7] One of them, *Morey v. Doud*,[8] involving economic interests, was plainly a sport. The other, *Skinner v. Oklahoma*[9]—the sterilization case—after lying dormant some twenty years, proved to be a viable seed in the Warren years.

A quasi blossoming came in the race cases beginning with *Brown v. Board of Education*.[10] Plainly they recognized that problems of racial differentiation were not to be resolved by the lenient standards that had prevailed in the *Kotch-Goesaert-*

Lee Optical line of cases. Yet the new, obviously stricter, test could not—in view of the background and early interpretation of the Fourteenth Amendment[11]—be deemed a typical activist exercise in judicial law-making. As Professor Philip B. Kurland put it:

> Indeed, in a way, Chief Justice Warren was wrong when he suggested in *Brown* that the Court could not turn back the clock. For the Court was doing exactly that. It was returning to a recognition of the central purpose of the Equal Protection Clause, to protect Negroes from discrimination at the hands of legislative, administrative, and judicial bodies controlled by white majorities.[12]

Even so, Brown et al. may have stimulated a revival of substantive equal protection. The judges could hardly have failed to notice the highly verbal enthusiasm of their main constituency (the intellectual community) for the desegregation decisions as well as the earlier efforts to extend the Bill of Rights to the states. Then why not grant the same preferred treatment to other "fundamental" interests beyond civil liberties? Mr. Justice Douglas had been pressing in this direction for years, as Professor Kenneth L. Karst has demonstrated in an *admiring* (and thus misleadingly entitled) essay on "Invidious Discrimination: Justice Douglas and the Return of the 'Natural Law-Due Process Formula' "[13]

A small break came with *Griffin v. Illinois*[14] in 1954 when a majority coalesced on the proposition that a state's requirement of transcripts in *all* criminal appeals could not be permitted to block appeal by one too poor to meet the uniform standard. This might well have been achieved via *procedural* due process—a relatively clear, narrow and therefore confining concept of ancient and honorable lineage. Indeed it was so achieved, but only in part. In a five to four decision, Mr. Justice Black—who (except in some suffrage cases) consistently opposed both substantive due process and substantive equal protection—based his plurality opinion *partly* on the latter. How the Douglas innovation worked its way into a Black opinion may some day be revealed; now it is a tantalizing mystery. Plainly, however, a majority could not be mustered to rest upon it alone! Some 64 years earlier procedural due process had served similarly to ease the way for substantive due process.[15]

Justices Reed, Burton, Minton and Harlan dissented, noting that the challenged measure did not (in any here relevant way) classify or differentiate. It applied equally to all who would appeal in criminal cases. Fate—not the state—had been less kind to some than to others.

Griffin was an intimation. The real break came with changes in personnel—Justices Frankfurter, Reed, Burton, and Minton (of the *Griffin* era) having been replaced by Justices Goldberg, Stewart, Brennan, and White. Thus in *Reynolds v. Sims*[16] the Court selected an interest (one-man-one-vote) which it deemed sufficiently "fundamental" to be protected by the new high standard explicit in the long dormant *Skinner* seed, and implicit in *Brown* and *Griffin*. There was no word whatsoever with respect to *Kotch, Goesaert,* etc. This is particularly interesting since in *Baker v. Carr*[17]—where some two years earlier the one-man-one-vote revolution began—the Court had insisted that apportionment did not present a political-question difficulty because "Judicial standards under the Equal Protection Clause are well developed and familiar . . ." Moreover in a concurring opinion in *Carr* Mr. Justice Douglas had gone out of his way to make clear that only the traditional standard was called for: "Universal equality is not the test; there is room for weighting [of votes]." In short the Warren Court assumed jurisdiction of apportionment cases on the ground that there was an established, traditional standard to guide decision, and then in *Sims* abandoned that standard in favor of another. The new approach holds that, if the Court labels an interest "fundamental," any measure impinging upon it "must be carefully and meticulously scrutinized." What was implicit in this was later made explicit, namely; unless such scrutiny reveals a "compelling"[18] state interest in support of the impinging act, it would be held invalid. *The Warren Court never found a state measure sufficiently compelling to override anything it deemed fundamental!*

What growth potential was there in the new "rigid scrutiny" (i.e., upper level) standard for equal protection cases? In suffrage matters it proved to be substantial. Step by step one-man-one-vote was extended to all legislative bodies except (for obvious pragmatic reasons) the United States Senate—as well as to special purpose elections[19] Similarly a number of voting-qualification and access-to-the-ballot measures fell by virtue of that strict scrutiny which is the heart of substantive equal protection.[20]

How far beyond the franchise cases was the Warren Court prepared to go in finding "fundamentalness" in interests not secured in the Bill of Rights or elsewhere in the Constitution? *Levy v. Louisiana*[21] involved a typical wrongful-death statute which permitted legitimate, but not unacknowledged illegitimate, children to recover damages for the tortious death of a parent. Equating the interest here involved (the mother child relationship) with the "fundamental" interests at stake in *Skinner, Harper,* and *Brown*, Mr. Justice Douglas, writing for the Court, struck down as irrational not the statute, but the exception[22]

It is of course elementary that there is no common law right of recovery in such cases. That right comes as a matter of grace by statute, and Louisiana (with most other states) had chosen to define the class of proper plaintiffs in terms of their legal, rather than some other, relationship to the deceased. Thus, for example, wives and legitimate, as well as other acknowledged, children are in one category, mistresses and unacknowledged bastards are in another. The difference between the Court and the legislature seems simply a policy difference as to what kind of relationship—legal, economic, biological, emotional, for examples—should justify a tort action by the survivor. Justices Harlan, Black, and Stewart observed in dissent:

> The Court ... rules that the State must base its arbitrary definition of the plaintiff class on biological rather than legal relationships. Exactly how this makes the Louisiana scheme even marginally more "rational" is not clear, for neither a biological relationship nor legal acknowledgment is indicative of the love or economic dependence that may exist between two persons.

Finally, in *Shapiro v. Thomson*, the Warren Court (but not the Chief Justice) found "the right to travel interstate" unduly impeded by a one-year residency requirement for welfare eligibility.[23]

> ... the traditional [equal protection] criteria do not apply in these cases. Since the classification here touches on the fundamental right of inter-state movement, its constitutionality must be judged by the stricter standard of whether it promotes a *compelling* state interest. Under this standard, the waiting period clearly violates the Equal Protection Clause.

Earlier in his opinion of the Court, Mr. Justice Brennan had intimated that "the ability of the families to obtain the very means to subsist" was constitutionally "fundamental." Apparently unable to pull a majority together on that proposition, he turned to the travel ploy.

Dissenting, Chief Justice Warren and his brother Black found that Congress could authorize under the Commerce Clause, and indeed had authorized, the travel restrictions in question. They also found the lower level equal protection standard relevant and satisfied. In a separate dissent, Mr. Justice Harlan reviewed the whole development of the new substantive equal protection gambit and what seemed to him its weaknesses.

The Burger Court—The 1969 and 1970 Terms

Drastic changes came with a new Chief, and later a new Associate, Justice. In an opinion by Mr. Justice Harlan, *Boddie v. Connecticut*[24] held that inability to pay ordinary court costs and related fees could not be permitted to bar an indigent's access to a divorce court. In contrast to *Griffin*, the decision turned not even in part on equal protection, but exclusively on the much more confining principles of *procedural* due process.[25] Mr. Justice Black dissented. Justices Douglas and Brennan sought to perpetuate the broader equal protection stance in a concurring opinion.

Labine v. Vincent[26] upheld a Louisiana inheritance statute that distinguished —as the *Levy* statue had—between illegitimate, and other, offspring. The Court, per Mr. Justice Black, found

> . . . nothing in the vague generalities of the equal protection and due process clauses which empowers this Court to nullify the deliberate choice of the elected representatives of the people of Louisiana. [The] statute clearly has a rational basis in view of Louisiana's interest in promoting family life . . .

Levy was neither overruled nor distinguished, though it is distinguishable. Plainly the Court was too divided to achieve a majority for either route. Yet it is note-worthy that the three dissenters in *Levy* (Justices Black, Stewart, and Harlan) now formed a majority with Chief Justice Burger and Mr. Justice Blackmun. Justices Douglas, Brennan, White and Marshall, dissenting, found in the Louisiana law only the "untenable and discredited prejudice of bygone centuries." Some may find in this an echo of the pre-1937 judicial intolerance that denied citizens the function of deciding for themselves what morality—be it laissez faire or paternalism —was, or was not, "untenable and discredited." The problem as usual is not what substantive conclusion is "correct," but who should make the choice.

A more obvious blow to Warren Court activism came in *Dandridge v. Williams.*[27] Applying the *traditional* test, a majority upheld a state AFDC program despite a maximum aid limit per family. It had been challenged for denying equal treatment for children simply because of the size of their families. The farflung importance of the case lay in the following repudiation of what the Warren Court had been hinting particularly in *Shapiro*:

> To be sure the cases cited [herein], and many others enunciating the traditional [i.e., lower level] standard under the Equal Protection Clause, have in the main involved state regulation of business and industry. The administration of public welfare assistance, by contrast, involves the most basic economic needs of impoverished human beings. We recognize the dramatically real factual difference between the cited cases and this one, but we can find no basis for applying a different constitutional standard.

The Court was careful not to repudiate, but to confine and clarify, substantive equal protection's new dual standard. Ignoring several recent decisions, the new majority limited high level review to racial classifications or those intruding upon "constitutionally protected freedom."

Mr. Justice Harlan, concurring, repudiated even the newly narrowed version of substantive equal protection:

Except with respect to racial classification, to which unique historical considerations apply, . . . I believe the constitutional provisions assuring equal protection of the laws impose a standard of rationality of classification, long applied in the decisions of this Court, that does not depend upon the nature of the . . . interest involved.

Justices Brennan and Marshall dissented bitterly on Equal Protection and statutory-conflict grounds. Strangely a Douglas dissent rested only on the latter. There was one vacancy on the bench, the Fortas seat not yet having been taken by Mr. Justice Blackmun.

Dandridge is particularly interesting because, responding to Warren Court activism, it resorts to something quite like Mr. Justice Black's *Adamson*[28] device vis-à-vis the willfulness of the nine-old-men. That is, it would "incorporate" into the equality clause for special protection *only* those interests which have a foundation in the Constitution itself.

This means, for example, that a religious or racial minority is entitled to *extraordinary* court protection that a poverty minority cannot expect. Thus *James v. Valtierra*[29] upheld a referendum requirement for *low-rent* public housing projects. The Warren Court had vetoed a similar requirement vis-à-vis *open* housing.[30] In each case "special burdens" fell on a minority group. The differentiating factor for the new Court was that the Constitution outlaws state racism; it does not outlaw poverty. Justices Brennan, Marshall, and (interestingly) Blackmun dissented in *Valtierra*. Mr. Justice Douglas did not participate in the decision, nor had he reached the constitutional issue in *Dandridge*. Could it be that he was troubled? After all he had long fought for "incorporation," the heart of which is (or was) to deny special constitutional protection to judges' policy preferences that are unknown to the Constitution.

It is crucial that while the new Court denies indigents high-level equal protection, it has been strikingly sensitive to their claims in procedural due process matters. Paralleling *Boddie, Goldberg v. Kelly*[31] requires a hearing prior to termination of aid to welfare claimants. The rationale of course is that for judges to insist upon common procedural niceties is quite different from judicial interference with substantive policy.

Three decisions at the end of the 1970-71 term seriously undermined the Warren Court's position on voting rights. In *Whitcomb v. Chavis*[32] a three-judge federal District Court had found illicit gerrymandering in a multi-member district system which, it found, "operated to minimize and cancel out the voting strength" of a black ghetto in Indianapolis. The area in question—Center Township—plainly was large enough to have representatives of its own in a single member system. Its voting record was heavily Democratic. The multimember district (Marion County) in which it lay was highly Republican. The trial court found that the

. . proportion of legislators with residences in the ghetto elected from 1960 to 1968 was less than the ghetto's proportion of the population, less than the proportion of legislators elected from Washington Township, a less populous [relatively wealthy, white] district, and less than the ghetto would likely have elected had the county consisted of single-member districts.

Reversing an order that would have imposed single-member districts, the Supreme Court held that multimember districts are not invalid *per se*, and that there was no evidence of their improper use in this case:[33]

Although we cannot be sure of the facts since the [trial] court ignored the question, it seems unlikely that the Democratic Party could afford to overlook the ghetto in slating its candidates. Clearly, in 1964—the one election which the Democrats won—the party slated and elected one senator and one representative from Center Township ghetto as well as one senator and four representatives from other parts of Center Township and two representatives from census tract 220, which was within the ghetto area described by plaintiff. Nor is there any indication that the party failed to slate candidates satisfactory to the ghetto in other years. Absent evidence or findings we are not sure, but it seems reasonable to infer that had the Democrats won all of the elections or even most of them, the ghetto would have had no justifiable complaints about representation. . . . If this is the proper view of this case, the failure of the ghetto to have legislative seats in proportion to its population emerges more as a function of losing elections than of built in bias against poor Negroes.

Plaintiffs had conceded "there was no basis for asserting that the legislative districts in Indiana were designed to dilute the votes of minorities." In short, the Court found no "invidious discrimination" *simpliciter*—as though it recognized no more than the traditional equal protection standard.

Of broader consequence was the rejection of the trial court's implicit view that "any group with distinctive interests must be represented in legislative halls, if it is numerous enough to command at least one seat and represents a majority living in an area sufficiently compact to constitute a single-member district."

The short of it is that we are unprepared to hold that district-based elections decided by plurality vote are unconstitutional in either single- or multi-member districts simply because the supporters of losing candidates have no legislative seats assigned to them.[34]

The opinion suggests that to support a gerrymander finding, the trial court would have had to examine such matters as "the actual influence of Marion County's delegation in the Indiana legislature," and the possibility of "recurring poor performance by Marion County's delegation in the Indiana legislature with respect to Center Township ghetto" for the purpose of discovering whether "any legislative skirmish . . . would have come out differently had Marion County been [subdivided into] single-member districts."

Believing such matters entirely outside the competence of federal courts, Mr. Justic Harlan voted for remand and dismissal:

> The suggestion implicit in the Court's opinion that appellees may ultimately prevail if they can make their record in these and like respects . . .
> is . . . a manifestation of frustration by a Court . . . trapped in the "political thicket" and . . . looking for a way out.[35]

Justices Douglas, Brennan, and Marshall, in dissent, agreed with the trial court and acknowledged what no member of the *Sims* majority had ever so openly recognized: "The question of gerrymandering is the other half of *Reynolds* v. *Sims*." In short, one-man-one-vote alone is about as functional as a bicycle without a second wheel. It requires merely that all gerrymandered (and other) districts be equal in size. This is no guarantee, and at best chance protection, against what the Warren Court called "diluted" votes.[36]

In this setting the dissenters came face-to-face with the majority's crucial problem. This they stated and "resolved" as follows:

> It is said that if we prevent racial gerrymandering to-day, we must prevent gerrymandering of any special interest group to-morrow, whether it be social, economic, or ideological. [We] do not agree. Our Constitution has a special thrust when it comes to voting; the Fifteenth Amendment says the right . . . to vote shall not be "abridged" on account of "race." . . .

The best then that the three heroes of the Warren era could do with what they recognized as "the other half of *"Reynolds* v. *Sims"* was to permit all voting inequalities except that based on race. Thus gerrymandering that "dilutes" the votes of workingmen or students, for example, would be permissible—*the dissenters having dropped substantive equal protection* (the Fourteenth Amendment basis of *Sims*) in favor of the race-oriented Fifteenth Amendment. Allowing most, i.e., all but "colored," votes to be "diluted" by gerrymander (while forbidding dilution by unequal numbers) is hardly the free choice of an ardent activist.

It is imposed by his recognition that—except with respect to race and numbers—the problem is too politically complex for courts. Presumably because this "compromise" entails gross discrimination against white voters, it was unacceptable to the majority. The crux of the difficulty is that interests are not homogenized. They are not spread uniformly throughout a state. Some are geographically compact; some attenuated; some disconnected. They overlap here and there in multiple, crazy-quilt patterns that defy geographic rationalization. It follows that any districting "fair" to one group inevitably is "unfair" to some or all others.[37]

Whitcomb then comes to this. The more "conservative" majority (Chief Justice Burger with Justices Black, Stewart, White, and Blackmun) still struggled in the well-known, yet intractable thicket. Mr. Justice Harlan chided them for staying there. The activist dissenters (Justices Douglas, Brennan, and Marshall)—acknowledging in effect that Justices Frankfurter and Harlan were essentially right in the first place[38]—confined their efforts to that small part of the apportionment issue which can be identified by color or numbers. Let others speculate on whether Warren and Fortas, J.J., could have been induced to take this position! For the Chief it would have meant a kind of coming together of what he must believe were his two major decisions—*Brown* v. *Board of Education* and *Reynolds* v. *Sims*.

The Burger Court's willingness to recognize political realities—whether or not it could handle them—was further revealed in *Abate* v. *Mundt*[39] and *Gordon* v. *Lance*.[40] The former—over dissents by Justices Douglas and Brennan—upheld an 11.9 per cent population variation among county legislative districts because of the need for flexibility in local government, the interest in preserving the integrity of political subdistrict boundary lines, and long standing tradition. The Warren Court had ignored all such pragmatic considerations and denounced a 5.97 per cent variation among congressional districts as excessive.[41] *Lance*, relying heavily on anti-majoritarian "federal analogy," upheld a law that gave opponents of school bond issues one-and-a-half times the voting power of proponents, since it discriminated merely against an abstract majority, not against any identifiable class.[42] Only Justices Brennan and Marshall dissented. It seemed to Mr. Justice Harlan that, abandoning the old regime's predilection for "majoritarianism as a rule of decision," the new Court ought to offer an alternative rationale—or retreat from the political arena.

Abate and *Lance* reject the Warren Court's simple arithmetic approach to complex political problems.[43] Relying on the more sophisticated mathematics of elementary probability theory, plaintiffs in *Whitcomb* offered "proof" of racial malappportionment. Finding this also ignored too many facts of political life, the Burger Court rested heavily on our long tradition of multimember districts and fear that "affirmance of the District Court would spawn endless litigation."

In several race and alienage cases, the Burger Court was *unanimous* in sustaining equal protection claims. Arizona and Pennsylvania had distinguished between citizens and aliens with respect to welfare benefits. Recognizing that "Under traditional equal protection principles, a State retains broad discretion to classify as long as its classification has a reasonable basis," the Justices repeated the *Dandridge* observation that this is so in the area of economics as well as in "social welfare" cases. "But the Court's decisions have established that classifications based on alienage, like those based on nationality, or race, are inherently suspect and subject to close judicial scrutiny."[44] Mr. Justice Harlan concurred, but only on the Court's "additional" ground of decision: conflict between state and national policy.

One thought more on the Burger Court. Its position on school desegregation was plainly "high level" and unanimous in *Alexander* v. *Holmes County Board of Education*[45] (the "immediate" desegregation case) and in *Swann* v. *Charlotte-Mecklenburg Board of Education*[46] (the busing case). No more (or less) could have been expected from the Warren Court. But, if the new regime did not retreat, neither did it advance to a new position on the race issue when invited to do so in *Palmer* v. *Thompson.*[47] When judicially ordered to desegregate its recreational facilities, Jackson Mississippi did so except with respect to its swimming pools. These it simply closed. The trial court found that the closing was "justified to preserve peace and order, and because the pools could not be operated economically on an integrated basis." The United States Court of Appeals for the Fifth Circuit—which has a proud record indeed in race cases—sitting *en banc* sustained by a seven to six vote the decision below against judicial intrusion. An opinion of the Court by Mr. Justice Black upheld that position, finding no inequality of treatment:

> In should be noted that neither the Fourteenth Amendment nor any act of Congress purports to impose an affirmative duty to . . . operate swimming pools. Furthermore, this is not a case where whites are permitted to use public facilities while blacks are denied access.

The best that Mr. Justice Douglas could do in dissent was to fall back on the utter vacuity of the Ninth Amendment and his earlier "penumbra" doctrine.[48] Justices Brennan, White, and Marshall joined the Douglas dissent, but stressed another approach. Repudiating the trial court's finding, they saw racial motivation in the city's conduct, and deemed that sufficient to tip the equal protection scale.

Conclusion

The Roosevelt Court abandoned one form of judicial activism, and toyed with another. Demolishing substantive due process and equal protection, it (more accurately some of its members) instigated the slow movement for incorporation of the Bill of Rights. Their efforts blossomed in the Warren era. But the Bill of Rights, after all, is quite old-fashioned. It does not contemplate many things deemed crucial in our day: poverty, universal equal suffrage, and birth control, for examples. At least by contrast to the Fourteenth Amendment (for which Holmes saw only the sky as a limit), the Bill of Rights is confining—too confining in any event for today's judicial activists. They tried to expand it by the "penumbra" theory and by appeal to the absolute void of the Ninth Amendment.[49] These efforts did not thrive. Return to nonprocedural due process was unthinkable; its unhappy history is still too vivid. Finally they found in equal protection the same opportunity for judicial legislation that the "nine old men" had found in substantive due process. A reaction was inevitable.

Mr. Justice Black's role in all this was crucial. Indeed, in a most basic sense it is his story. He could not abide doctrines that allow judges to impose their own predilections upon a reluctant community. Thus no one surpassed his early efforts to destroy substantive due process and substantive equal protection. At the same time he led the movement to incorporate the Bill of Rights into the Fourteenth Amendment. Obviously these were complementary efforts directed at the same target; judicial free wheeling. Believing deeply in government by law and not by men, he would read all of the old judge-made accretions out of that most ambiguous of amendments, and replace them exlusively with the essence of the Bill of Rights. There his Fourteenth Amendment activism stopped. Indeed, for him, this was not activism.[50] For he had convinced himself, if few others, that a historic purpose of the Fourteenth Amendment was to impose Bill-of-Rights limitations upon the states.[51] In his view, those limitations—unlike the amorphous substantive due process and equal protection doctrines—provided "clearly marked ... boundaries"[52] to guide decision and foreclose judicial fiat. Given this special court protection for the basic civil rights and civil liberties, he could find no other meaning in democracy than this: The people must be free to formulate their own policies on poverty, birth control,[53] and other social issues—however wise or unwise they may seem to judges. It comes at last to this: Courts must protect "fundamental" interests, but in determining what is fundamental they must look to the Constitution.

The subjectivity of the Warren Court's determinations in this area cannot be hidden. It used the stringent test in most suffrage cases,[54] but not vis-à-vis a statute that denied ballots to jailees; not vis-à-vis higher criminal penalties for habitual criminals than for others,[55] and not in a freedom of religion controversy.[56] Even Mr. Justice Black on occasion ran afoul of his own guidelines. A leader of the one-man-one-vote revolution, he dissented bitterly in the poll tax case (charging that the Court had returned to the old "natural law due process" formula). In short he accepted the high-level test in *Sims* and *Lucas*, but not in *Harper*.[57] A related difficulty of substantive equal protection, as its chief academic sponsor recognizes, is that "Since most legislation has differential effects on various groups, discrimination . . . can be found [or ignored] in almost anything the legislature does—or fails to do."[58] The courts then end up (as in the old days) with a general power to supervise virtually the whole sphere of government.[59] The result is likely to be what we had in the first third of this century: government by the judiciary, as one observer described it.

If the equality principle is to go beyond its historic purpose of protection against governmental racism, the traditional, single standard (in nonrace cases) seemed to the late Mr. Justice Harlan our best hope for equal application of the equal protection clause. It "reduces to a minimum the likelihood that the federal judiciary will judge state policies in terms of the individual notions and predilections of its members . . ."[60] Mr. Justice Harlan perhaps had more reason than most of us to remember *inter alia* the blunder of the *Sewer Pipe Case*[61] in which his grandfather wrote for the Court—to say nothing of the first Mr. Justice Harlan's views in *Cumming* v. *Richmond*[62] and *Berea College* v. *Kentucky*.[63]

Remembering too, no doubt, the early Burger Court—like the Roosevelt Court—repudiated much of the equal protection activism of its predecessor. Yet it went beyond Mr. Justice Harlan by recognizing a special status under the equality clause for constitutionally grounded interests, and only those interests. President Nixon's campaign for "strict construction" seems to have had some effect! So did President Roosevelt's similar efforts a generation ago. In those days, however, we spoke not of strict construction but of a "return to the Constitution."

The great question now is this: Will the full Nixon Court keep these early counsels of restraint? Or will it too succumb to the magic of power, and give high-level protection to interests which *it* deems fundamental? If the latter alternative is to be our fate, some of us may find embarrassment in our quondam efforts to convince ourselves that judicial activism (it used to be called judicial supremacy) is a proper handmaiden of democracy. We may even come to wonder—as liberals generally have until recently—whether there is any democratic justification whatsoever for a nonelected superlegislature that pretends to be a court.

In the year following the departure of Justices Black and Harlan (and the writing of the above) the Court seems to have adopted a new tack. At least when "constitutionally grounded freedom" is not at stake, recent equal-protection decisions suggest a balancing of interests approach that necessarily rejects both the Roosevelt Court's "abdication" in nonrace cases and the "activism" of the Warren era. See particularly, *Weber* v. *Aetna*, 92 S. Ct. 1400 (1972); *Lindsey* v. *Norment*, 92 S. Ct. 862 (1972); *Reed* v. *Reed*, 92 S. Ct. 251 (1971).

FOOTNOTES

[1] *Connolly* v. *Union Sewer Pipe Co.*, 184 U.S. 540 (1902).

[2] 257 U.S. 312 (1921).

[3] *Kotch* v. *Bd. of River Port Pilots Comm'rs*, 330 U.S. 552 (1947).

[4] *Goesaert* v. *Cleary*, 335 U.S. 464 (1948).

[5] *Williamson* v. *Lee Optical Co.*, 348 U.S. 483 (1955).

[6] This expression of the traditional view actually comes from Chief Justice Warren's opinion of the Court in *McGowan* v. *Maryland*, 366 U.S. 420, 425-426 (1961). It is an outline of an extended statement in *Morey* v. *Doud*, 354 U.S. 457, 463-464 (1957).

[7] Excluded here are cases in which state measures were stricken down because of their extraterritorial effects. These of course involve the old problem of "taxation [or regulation] without representation," and thus come within the Roosevelt Court's special concern for the processes of popular self-government. See, for example, *Southern Pacific* v. *Arizona*, 325 U.S. 761 (1945).

[8] Cited in fn. 6.

[9] 316 U.S. 535 (1942).

[10] 347 U.S. 483 (1954).

[11] For example, *Slaughter House Cases*, 16 Wall. 36 (1873); *Strauder* v. *West Virginia*, 100 U.S. 303 (1880).

[12] *Politics, the Constitution, and the Supreme Court* (Chicago:The University of Chicago Press, 1970), pp. 110-111.

[13] UCLA LAW REVIEW 716 (1969).

[14] 351 U.S. 12 (1956).

[15] *Chicago, M. & St. P. R. Co.* v. *Minnesota*, 134 U.S. 418 (1890) is generally considered the beginning of the flood of substantive due process cases. The Court's opinion rests in part on procedural considerations.

[16] 377 U.S. 533 (1964).

[17] 369 U.S. 186 (1962).

[18] See, for example, *Williams* v. *Rhodes*, 393 U.S. 23 (1968). For the Warren Court's own comparison of the traditional and the new tests, see *McDonald* v. *Bd. of Election of Chicago*, 394 U.S. 802, 807-809 (1969). The "careful scrutiny" rule is used also in case of "suspect classifications." See note 44 and related text, below.

[19] *Avery* v. *Midland County*, 390 U.S. 474 (1968); *Hadley* v. *Junior College District*, 397 U.S. 50 (1970); *Kramer* v. *Union Free School District*, 395 U.S. 621 (1969); *Cipriano* v. *City of Houma*, 395 U.S. 701 (1969).

[20] For example, *Carrington* v. *Rash*, 380 U.S. 89 (1965); *Harper* v. *Virginia Bd. of Elections*, 383 U.S. 663 (1966); *Williams* v. *Rhodes*, 393 U.S. 23 (1968).

[21] 391 U.S. 68 (1968).

[22] In *Connolly* v. *Union Sewer Pipe Co.* (cited in fn. 1) the "old Court" found invidious discrimination in a state antitrust law which covered businessmen but not farmers. It struck down not the "bad" exception but the whole measure! This and the opposite tactic in *Levy* demonstrate a crucial phase of judicial activism.

[23] 394 U.S. 618, 638 (1969).

[24] 91 S.Ct. 780 (1971).

[25] Prior to the new poverty-procedural-due-process approach in *Boddie*, the Burger Court unanimously invalidated on equal protection grounds two state laws which would incarcerate indigents (unable "forthwith to pay a fine in full") when others could escape that fate by virtue of fiscal competence. The first of these—*Williams* v. *Illinois*, 399 U.S. 235 (1970)—rested simply on *Griffin* v. *Illinois* (cited in fn. 14). The opinion in the second, *Tate* v. *Short*, 91 S.Ct. 668 (1971) was singularly laconic, marking presumably the soon to be accomplished transition to *Boddie*.

[26] 91 S.Ct. 1017 (1971).

[27] 397 U.S. 471 (1970).

[28] *Adamson* v. *California*, 332 U.S. 46, 68 (1947).

[29] 91 S.Ct. 1331 (1971).

[30] *Hunter* v. *Erickson*, 393 U.S. 385 (1969).

[31] 397 U.S. 254 (1970).

[32] 91 S.Ct. 1858 (1971).

[33] Pp. 1872-1874.

[34] P. 1878.

[35] P. 1883.

[36] See Ward Elliott, "Prometheus, Proteus, Pandora, and Procrustes Unbound: The Political Consequences of Reapportionment," 37 THE UNIVERSITY OF CHICAGO LAW REVIEW 474 (1970); Wallace Mendelson, "Book Review," 58 GEORGETOWN LAW JOURNAL 435 (1969).

[37] Mendelson.

[38] See their dissenting opinions in *Baker* v. *Carr* (cited in fn. 17).

[39] 91 S.Ct. 1904 (1971).

[40] 91 S.Ct. 1889 (1971).

[41] *Kirkpatrick* v. *Preisler*, 394 U.S. 526 (1969). The Warren Court had said that justifiable deviations from mathematical equality would be permitted, but it never found any it deemed justifiable.

[42] Cf. the two-thirds majority requirement for impeachment and treaty ratification in the federal Constitution. The lower court had relied mistakenly, as it turned out, on *Gray* v. *Sanders*, 372 U.S. 368 (1963) and *Cipriano* v. *City of Houma*, 395 U.S. 701 (1969).

[43] This seems to be the new trend also among scholars. See, for example, Robert G. Dixon, *Democratic Representation: Reapportionment in Law and Politics* (New York: Oxford University Press, 1968), pp. 544 *et seq.*; Thomas R. Dye, *Politics, Economics and the Public* (Chicago: Rand McNally, 1966) p. 280; Elliott, "Prometheus . . . " (cited in fn. 36).

[44] *Graham* v. *Richardson* and *Sailer* v. *Leger*, 91 S.Ct. 1848, 1852 (1971). Cf. *Rogers* v. *Bellei*, 91 S.Ct. 1060 (1971).

[45] 396 U.S. 19 (1969).

[46] 91 S.Ct. 1267 (1971).

[47] 91 S.Ct. 1940 (1971). See also *Griggs* v. *Duke Power Co.*, 91 S.Ct. 849 (1971). It is arguable that the Warren Court's position in *Griffin* v. *Prince Edwards County*, 377 U.S. 218 (1964) and *Orleans Parish School District* v. *Bush*, 365 U.S. 569 (1961), required a different result in *Palmer.*

[48] See his opinion in *Griswold* v. *Connecticut*, 381 U.S. 479, 484 (1965).

[49] *Griswold* v. *Connecticut.*

[50] He saw "incorporation" as an antiactivist device. Apart from the problem of racism, it was calculated to confine the Fourteenth Amendment to a Bill of Rights meaning.

[51] The literature on this problem is extensive. Some of it is covered in Wallace Mendelson, "Mr. Justice Black's Fourteenth Amendment," 53 MINNESOTA LAW REVIEW 711 (1969).

[52] *FPC* v. *Natural Gas Pipeline Co.*, 315 U.S. 575, 601, note 4 (1942).

[53] The poverty cases are discussed above. As to birth control, see his biting dissent in *Griswold* v. *Connecticut* (cited in fn. 48).

[54] See cases cited in fns. 16, 18-20.

[55] *Oyler* v. *Boles*, 368 U.S. 448 (1962); *McDonald* v. *Bd. of Election Comm'rs*, 394 U.S. 802 (1969).

[56] *McGowan* v. *Maryland*, 366 U.S. 420 (1961).

[57] The crux of Mr. Justice Black's problem was that his dedication to democracy dictated special court protection for the suffrage, though suffrage is not covered in the Bill of Rights. Writing the Court's first one-man-one-vote opinion he carefully avoided reliance upon equal protection. *Wesberry* v. *Sanders*, 376 U.S. 1 (1964). Then he silently, and no doubt painfully, went along with the Court's substantive equal protection approach in *Sims et al.* In *Harper* he returned to type, but it was too late. *Griswold* a few months earlier had already emasculated his quarter century effort to tame the Fourteenth Amendment. The Court's effort in that case to tie birth control into the Bill of Rights, if designed to placate the Justice, can only be deemed an insult to his intelligence. As he forcefully pointed out, the Court had simply put new garments on the old due process wolf. For Mr. Justice Black the lesson of *Sims* must have been this: The role of demi-virgin is not easily maintained.

[58] Karst, "Invidious Discrimination . . . " p. 740.

[59] Including, as Karst would have it (see quotation at note 58, above) governmental nonaction. Since equal protection is included in the Fifth Amendment (at least for some purposes, *Bolling* v. *Shape*, 347 U.S. 497 [1954], the supervisory power would extend to the federal government as well as to the states.

[60] Mr. Justice Harlan dissenting in *Harper* v. *Virginia Bd. of Elections* (cited in fn. 20) pp. 681-682.

[61] Cited in fn. 1, above.

[62] 175 U.S. 528 (1899).

[63] 211 U.S. 45 (1908).

CHAPTER 2   "The Wages of Crying Wolf: A Comment on *Roe v. Wade*"*

JOHN HART ELY**

Wallace Mendelson concludes the previous selection by posing the question: "Will the full Nixon Court keep these early counsels of self-restraints? Or will it too succumb to the magic of power . . . ?"

Less than a year after Mendelson's article was published, his question was answered, at least for some, when the Court announced its decisions in *Roe v. Wade* and *Doe v. Bolton* (1973), the abortion cases. Justice White put it bluntest, perhaps, when he labelled the majority opinion of Justice Harry Blackmun "an exercise of raw judicial power."

The abortion decisions, aside from the emotions they generate and continue to generate, are the best examples of the paradox so often presented by the Burger Court. On the one hand, support for abortion increasingly appears to have emerged as one of the touchstones for modern liberalism. On the other hand, as Professor John Hart Ely notes in the following article, the Court's opinion in *Roe* and *Doe* seems in many respects to represent a return to a discredited jurisprudence of an earlier era, to *Lochner v. New York* (1905), and to a judiciary that was anything but liberal.

Certain of the ideas first presented by Professor Ely in this article are developed in more detail in his recent treatise on judicial review, *Democracy and Distrust*, published in 1980 by the Harvard University Press.

*Reprinted without footnotes from 82 *Yale Law Review* (1973), pp. 920-949. © 1973 by John Hart Ely
**Professor of Law, Harvard Law School

• • • • • •

The interests of the mother and the fetus are opposed. On which side should the State throw its weight? The issue is volatile; and it is resolved by the moral code which an individual has.

In *Roe v. Wade,* decided January 22, 1973, the Supreme Court—Justice Blackmun speaking for everyone but Justices White and Rehnquist—held unconstitutional Texas's (and virtually every other state's) criminal abortion statute. The broad outlines of its argument are not difficult to make out:

1. The right to privacy, though not explicitly mentioned in the Constitution, is protected by the Due Process Clause of the Fourteenth Amendment.

2. This right "is broad enough to encompass a woman's decision whether or not to terminate her pregnancy."

3. This right to an abortion is "fundamental" and can therefore be regulated only on the basis of a "compelling" state interest.

4. The state does have two "important and legitimate" interests here, the first in protecting maternal health, the second in protecting the life (or potential life) of the fetus. But neither can be counted "compelling" throughout the entire pregnancy: Each matures with the unborn child.

These interests are separate and distinct. Each grows in substantiality as the woman approaches term and, at a point during pregnancy, each becomes "compelling."

5. During the first trimester of pregnancy, neither interest is sufficiently compelling to justify any interference with the decision of the woman and her physician. Appellants have referred the Court to medical data indicating that mortality rates for women undergoing early abortions, where abortion is legal, "appear to be as low as or lower than the rates for normal childbirth." Thus the state's interest in protecting maternal health is not compeling during the first trimester. Since the interest in protecting the fetus is not yet compelling either, during the first trimester the state can neither prohibit an abortion nor regulate the conditions under which one is performed.

6. As we move into the second trimester, the interest in protecting the fetus remains less than compelling, and the decision to have an abortion thus continues to control. However, at this point the health risks of abortion begin to exceed those of childbirth. "It follows that, from and after this point, a State may regulate the abortion procedure to the extent that the regulation reasonably relates to the preservation and protection of maternal health." Abortion may not be prohibited during the second trimester, however.

7. At the point at which the fetus becomes viable the interest in protecting it becomes compelling, and therefore from that point on the state can prohibit abortions *except*—and this limitation is also apparently a constitutional command, though it receives no justification in the opinion—when they are necessary to protect maternal life or health.

A number of fairly standard criticisms can be made of *Roe.* A plausible narrower basis of decision that of vagueness, is brushed aside in the rush toward broader ground. The opinion strikes the reader initially as a sort of guidebook, addressing questions not before the Court and drawing lines with an apparent precision one generally associates with a commissioner's regulations. On closer examination, however, the precision proves largely illusory. Confusing signals are emitted, particularly with respect to the nature of the doctor's responsibilities and the permissible scope of health regulations after the first trimester. The Court seems, moreover, to get carried away on the subject of remedies: Even assuming the case can be made for an unusually protected constitutional right to an abortion, it hardly seems necessary to have banned during the first trimester *all* state regulation of the conditions under which abortions can be performed.

By terming such criticisms "standard," I do not mean to suggest they are unimportant, for they are not. But if they were all that was wrong with *Roe*, it would not merit special comment.

Let us not underestimate what is at stake: Having an unwanted child can go a long way toward ruining a woman's life. And at bottom *Roe* signals the Court's judgment that this result cannot be justified by any good that anti-abortion legislation accomplishes. This surely is an understandable condition—indeed it is one with which I agree—but ordinarily the Court claims no mandate to second-guess legislative balances, at least not when the Constitution has designated neither of the values in conflict as entitled to special protection. But even assuming it would be a good idea for the Court to assume this function, *Roe* seems a curious place to have begun. Laws prohibiting the use of "soft" drugs or, even more obviously, homosexual acts between consenting adults can stunt "the preferred life styles" of those against whom enforcement is threatened in very serious ways. It is clear such acts harm no one besides the participants, and indeed the case that the participants are harmed is a rather shaky one. Yet such laws survive, on the theory that there exists a "societal consensus" that the behavior involved is revolting or at any rate immoral. Of course the consensus is not universal but it is sufficient, and this is what is counted crucial, to get the laws passed and keep them on the books. Whether anti-abortion legislation cramps the life style of an unwilling mother more significantly than anti-homosexuality legislation cramps the life style of a homosexual is a close question. But even granting that it does, the *other* side of the balance looks very different. For there is more than simple societal revulsion to support legislation restricting abortion: Abortion ends (or if it makes a difference, prevents) the life of a human being other than the one making the choice.

The Court's response here is simply not adequate. It agrees, indeed it holds, that after the point of viability (a concept it fails to note will become even less clear than it is now as the technology of birth continues to develop) the interest in protecting the fetus is compelling. Exactly why that is the magic moment is not made clear: Viability, as the Court defines it, is achieved some six to twelve weeks after quickening. (Quickening is the point at which the fetus begins discernibly to move independently of the mother and the point that has historically been deemed crucial—to the extent *any* point between conception and birth has been focused on.) But no, it is *viability* that is constitutionally critical: the Court's defense seems to mistake a definition for a syllogism.

> With respect to the State's important and legitimate interest in poten-
> tial life, the "compelling" point is at viability. This is so because the
> fetus then presumably has the capacity of meaningful life outside the
> mother's womb.

With regard to why the state cannot consider this "important and legitimate inter-est" prior to viability, the opinion is even less satisfactory. The discussion begins sensibly enough: The interest asserted is not necessarily tied to the question whether the fetus is "alive," for whether or not one calls it a living being, it is an entity with the potential for (and indeed the likelihood of) life. But all of arguable rele-vance that follows are arguments that fetuses (a) are not recognized as "persons in the whole sense" by legal doctrine generally and (b) are not "persons" pro-tected by the Fourteenth Amendment.

To the extent they are not entirely inconclusive, the bodies of doctrine to which the Court adverts respecting the protection of fetuses under general legal doctrine tend to undercut rather than support its conclusion. And the argu-ment that fetuses (unlike say, corporations) are not "persons" under the Four-teenth Amendment fares little better. The Court notes that most constitutional clauses using the word "persons"—such as the one outlining the qualifications for the Presidency—appear to have been drafted with postnatal beings in mind. (It might have added that most of them were plainly drafted with *adults* in mind, but I suppose that wouldn't have helped.) In addition, "the appellee conceded on reargument that no case can be cited that holds that a fetus is a person within the meaning of the Fourteenth Amendment." (The other legal contexts in which the question could have arisen are not enumerated.)

The cannons of construction employed here are perhaps most intriguing when they are contrasted with those invoked to derive the constitutional right to an abortion. But in any event, the argument that fetuses lack constitutional rights is simply irrelevant. For it has never been held or even asserted that the state interest needed to justify forcing a person to refrain from an activity, *whether or not that activity is constitutionally protected,* must implicate either the life or the constitutional rights of another person. Dogs are not "persons in the whole sense" nor have they constitutional rights, but that does not mean the state cannot prohibit killing them: It does not even mean the state cannot prohibit killing them in the exercise of the First Amendment right of political protest. Come to think of it, draft cards aren't persons either.

Thus even assuming the Court ought generally to get into the business of second-guessing legislative balances, it has picked a strange case with which to begin. Its purported evaluation of the balance that produced anti-abortion legislation simply does not meet the issue: That the life plans of the mother must, not simply may, prevail over the state's desire to protect the fetus simply does not follow from the judgment that the fetus is not a person. Beyond all that, however, the Court has no business getting into that business.

*

Were I a legislator I would vote for a statute very much like the one the Court ends up drafting. I hope this reaction reflects more than the psychological phenomenon that keeps bombardiers sane—the fact that it is somehow easier to "terminate" those you cannot see—and am inclined to think it does: that the mother, unlike the unborn child, has begun to imagine a future for herself strikes me as morally quite significant. But God knows I'm not *happy* with that resolution. Abortion is too much like infanticide on the one had, and too much like contraception on the other, to leave one comfortable with any answer; and the moral issue it poses is as fiendish as any philosopher's hypothetical.

Of course, the Court often resolves difficult moral questions, and difficult questions yield controversial answers. I doubt, for example, that most people would agree that letting a drug peddler go unapprehended is morally preferable to letting the police kick down his door without probable cause. The difference, of course, is that the Constitution, which legitimates and theoretically controls judicial intervention, has some rather pointed things to say about this choice. There will of course be difficult questions about the applicability of its language to specific facts, but at least the document's special concern with one of the values in conflict is manifest. It simply says nothing, clear or fuzzy, about abortion.

The matter cannot end there, however. The Burger Court, like the Warren Court before it has been especially solicitous of the right to travel from state to state, demanding a compelling state interest if it is to be inhibited. Yet nowhere in the Constitution is such a right mentioned. It is, however, as clear as such things can be that this right was one the framers intended to protect, most specifically by the

Privileges and Immunities Clause of Article IV. The right is, moreover, plausibly inferable from the system of government, and the citizen's role therein, contemplated by the Constitution. The Court in *Roe* suggests an inference of neither sort—from the intent of the framers, or from the governmental system contemplated by the Constitution—in support of the constitutional right to an abortion.

What the Court does assert is that there is a general right of privacy granted special protection—that is, protection above and beyond the baseline requirement of "rationality"—by the Fourteenth Amendment, and that that right "is broad enough to encompass" the right to an abortion. The general right of privacy is inferred, as it was in *Griswold v. Connecticut*, from various provisions of the Bill of Rights manifesting a concern with privacy, notably the Fourth Amendment's guarantee against unreasonable searches, the Fifth Amendment's privilege against self-incrimination, and the right, inferred from the First Amendment, to keep one's political associations secret.

One possible response is that all this proves is that the things explicitly mentioned are forbidden, if indeed it does not actually demonstrate a disposition *not* to enshrine anything that might be called a general right of privacy. In fact the Court takes this view when it suits its purposes. (On the *same day* it decided *Roe*, the Court held that a showing of reasonableness was not needed to force someone to provide a grand jury with a voice exemplar, reasoning that the Fifth Amendment was not implicated because the evidence was not "testimonial" and that the Fourth Amendment did not apply because there was no "seizure.") But this approach is unduly crabbed. Surely the Court is entitled, indeed I think it is obligated, to seek out the sorts of evils the framers meant to combat and to move against their twentieth century counterparts.

Thus it seems to me entirely proper to infer a general right of privacy, *so long as some care is taken in defining the sort of right the inference will support.* Those aspects of the First, Fourth and Fifth Amendments to which the Court refers all limit the ways in which, and the circumstances under which, the government can go about gathering information about a person he would rather it did not have. *Katz v. United States*, limiting governmental tapping of telephones, may not involve what the framers would have called a "search," but it plainly involves this general concern with privacy. *Griswold* is a long step, even a leap, beyond this, but at least the connection is discernible. Had it been a case that purported to discover in the Constitution a "right to contraception," it would have been *Roe's* strongest precedent. But the Court in *Roe* gives no evidence of so regarding it, and rightly not. Commentators tend to forget, though the Court plainly has not, that the Court in *Griswold* stressed that it was invalidating only that portion of the Connecticut law that proscribed the *use*, as opposed to the manufacture, sale, or other distribution of contraceptives. That distinction (which would be silly were the right to contraception being constitutionally enshrined) makes sense if the case is rationalized on the ground that the section of the law whose constitutionality was in issue was such that *its enforcement would have been virtually impossible without* the most outrageous sort of governmental prying into the privacy of the home. And this, indeed, is the theory on which the Court appeared rather explicitly to settle:

> The present case, then, concerns a relationship lying within the zone of privacy created by several fundamental constitutional guarantees. And it concerns a law which, in forbidding the *use* of contraceptives rather than regulating their manufacture or sale, seeks to achieve its goals by means having a maximum destructive impact upon that relationship. Such a law cannot stand in light of the familiar principle, so often applied by this Court, that "a governmental purpose to control or prevent activities constitutionally subject to state regulation may not be achieved by means which sweep unnecessarily broadly and thereby invade the area of protected freedoms." *NAACP v. Alabama,* 377 U.S. 288, 307. Would we allow the police to search the sacred precincts of marital bedrooms for telltale signs of the use of contraceptives? The very idea is repulsive to the notions of privacy surrounding the marriage relationship.

Thus even assuming (as the Court surely seemed to) that a state can constitutionally seek to minimize or eliminate the circulation and use of contraceptives, Connecticut had acted unconstitutionally by selecting a means, that is a direct ban on use, that would generate intolerably intrusive modes of data-gathering. No such rationalization is attempted by the Court in *Roe*—and understandably not, for whatever else may be involved, it is not a case about governmental snooping.

The Court reports that some amici curiae argued for an unlimited right to do as one wishes with one's body. This theory holds, for me at any rate, much appeal. However, there would have been serious problems with its invocation in this case. In the first place, more than the mother's own body is involved in a decision to have an abortion; a fetus may not be a "person in the whole sense," but it is certainly not nothing. Second, it is difficult to find a basis for thinking that the theory was meant to be given constitutional sanction: Surely it is no part of the "privacy" interest the Bill of Rights suggests.

> [I]t is not clear to us that the claim ... that one has an unlimited right to do with one's body as one pleases bears a close relationship to the right of privacy ...

Unfortunately, having thus rejected the amici's attempt to define the bounds of the general constitutional right of which the right to an abortion is a part, on the theory that the general right described has little to do with privacy, the Court provides neither an alternative definition nor an account of why *it* thinks privacy is involved. It simply announces that the right to privacy "is broad enough to encompass a woman's decision whether or not to terminate her pregnancy." Apparently this conclusion is thought to derive from the passage that immediately follows it:

> The detriment that the State would impose upon the pregnant woman by denying this choice altogether is apparent. Specific and direct harm medically diagnosable even in early pregnancy may be involved. Maternity, or additional offspring, may force upon the woman a distressful life and future. Psychological harm may be imminent. Mental and physical health may be taxed by child care. There is also the distress, for all concerned, associated with the unwanted child, and there is the problem of bringing a child into a family already unable, psychologically and otherwise, to care for it. In other cases, as in this one, the additional difficulties and continuing stigma of unwed motherhood may be involved.

All of this is true and ought to be taken very seriously. But it has nothing to do with privacy in the Bill of Rights sense or any other the Constitution suggests. I suppose there is nothing to prevent one from using the word "privacy" to mean the freedom to live one's life without governmental interference. But the Court obviously does not so use the term. Nor could it, for such a right is at stake in *every* case. Our life styles are constantly limited, often seriously, by governmental regulation; and while many of us would prefer less direction, granting that desire the status of a preferred constitutional right would yield a system of "government" virtually unrecognizable to us and only slightly more recognizable to our forefathers. The Court's observations concerning the serious, life-shaping costs of having a child prove what might to the thoughtless have seemed unprovable: That even though a human life, or a potential human life, hangs in the balance, the moral dilemma abortion poses is so difficult as to be heartbreaking. What they fail to do is even begin to resolve that dilemma so far as our govermental system is concerned by associating either side of the balance with a value inferable from the Constitution.

But perhaps the inquiry should not end even there. In his famous *Carolene Products* footnote, Justice Stone suggested that the interests to which the Court can responsibly give extraordinary constitutional protection include not only those expressed in the Constitution but also those that are unlikely to receive adequate consideration in the political process, specifically the interests of "discrete and insular minorities" unable to form effective political alliances. There can be little doubt that such considerations have influenced the direction, if only occasionally the rhetoric, of the recent Courts. My repeated efforts to convince my students that sex should be treated as a "suspect classification" have convinced me it is no easy matter to state such considerations in a "principled" way. But passing that problem, *Roe* is not an appropriate case for their invocation.

Compared with men, very few women sit in our legislatures, a fact I believe should bear some relevance—even without an Equal Rights Amendment—to the appropriate standard of review for legislation that favors men over women. But *no* fetuses sit in our legislatures. Of course they have their champions, but so have women. The two interests have clashed repeatedly in the political arena, and had continued to do so up to the date of the opinion, generating quite a wide variety of accommodations. By the Court's lights virtually all of the legislative accommodations had unduly favored fetuses; by its definition of victory, women had lost. Yet in every legislative balance one of the competing interests loses to some extent; indeed usually, as here, they both do. On some occasions the Constitution throws its weight on the side of one of them, indicating the balance must be restruck. And on others—and this is Justice Stone's suggestion—it is at least arguable that, constitutional directive or not, the Court should throw *its* weight on the side of a minority demanding in court more than it was able to achieve politically. But even assuming this suggestion can be given principled content, it was clearly intended and should be reserved for those interests which, *as compared with the interests to which they have been subordinated,* constitute minorities unusually incapable of protecting themselves. Compared with men, women may constitute such a "minority"; compared with the unborn, they do not. I'm not sure I'd know a discrete and insular minority if I saw one, but confronted with a multiple choice question requiring me to designate (a) women or (b) fetuses as one, I'd expect no credit for the former answer.

Of course a woman's freedom to choose an abortion is part of the "liberty" the Fourteenth Amendment says shall not be denied without due process of law, as indeed is anyone's freedom to do what he wants. But "due process" generally guarantees only that the inhibition be procedurally fair and that it have some "rational" connection—though plausible is probably a better word—with a permissible governmental goal. What is unusual about *Roe* is that the liberty involved is accorded a far more stringent protection, so stringent that a desire to preserve the fetus's existence is unable to overcome it—a protection more stringent, I think it fair to say, than that the present Court accords the freedom of the press explicitly guaranteed by the First Amendment. What is frightening about *Roe* is that this super-protected right is not inferable from the language of the Constitution, the framers' thinking respecting the specific problem in issue, any general value derivable from the provisions they included, or the nation's governmental structure. Nor is it explainable in terms of the unusual political impotence of the group judicially protected vis-à-vis the interest that legislatively prevailed over it. And that, I believe—the predictable early reaction to *Roe* notwithstanding ("more of the same Warren-type activism")—is a charge that can responsibly be leveled at no other decision of the past twenty years. At times the inferences the Court has drawn from the values the Constitution marks for special protection have been controversial, even shaky, but never before has its sense of an obligation to draw one been so obviously lacking.

IV

Not in the last thirty-five years at any rate. For, as the received learning has it, this sort of thing did happen before, repeatedly. From its 1905 decision in *Lochner v. New York* into the 1930's the Court, frequently though not always under the rubric of "liberty of contract," employed the Due Process Clauses of the Fourteenth and Fifth Amendments to invalidate a good deal of legislation. According to the dissenters at the time and virtually all the commentators since, the Court had simply manufactured a constitutional right out of whole cloth and used it to superimpose its own view of wise social policy on those of the legislatures. So indeed the Court itself came to see the matter, and its reaction was complete:

> There was a time when the Due Process Clause was used by this Court to strike down laws which were thought unreasonable, that is, unwise or incompatible with some particular economic or social philosophy. In this manner the Due Process Clause was used, for example, to nullify laws prescribing maximum hours for work in bakeries, *Lochner v. New York*, 198 U.S. 45 (1905), outlawing "yellow dog" contracts, *Coppage v. Kansas*, 236 U.S. 1 (1915), setting minimum wages for women, *Adkins v. Children's Hospital*, 261 U.S. 525 (1923), and fixing the weight of loaves of bread, *Jay Burns Baking Co. v. Bryan*, 264 U.S. 504 (1924). This intrusion by the judiciary into the realm of legislative value judgments was strongly objected to at the time . . . Mr. Justice Holmes said,
>
> > "I think the proper course is to recognize that a state legislature can do whatever it sees fit to do unless it is restrained by some express prohibition in the Constitution of the United States or of the State, and that Courts should be careful not to extend such prohibitions beyond their obvious meaning by reading into them conceptions of public policy that the particular Court may happen to entertain."
>
> . . . The doctrine that prevailed in *Lochner, Coppage, Adkins, Burns,* and like cases—that due process authorizes courts to hold laws unconstitutional when they believe the legislature has acted unwisely—

has long since been discarded. We have returned to the original constitutional proposition that courts do not substitute their social and economic beliefs for the judgment of legislative bodies, who are elected to pass laws.

It may be objected that *Lochner et al.* protected the "economic rights" of businessmen whereas *Roe* protects a "human right." It should be noted, however, that not all of the *Lochner* series involved economic regulation; that even those that did resist the "big business" stereotype with which the commentators tend to associate them; and that in some of them the employer's "liberty of contract" claim was joined by the employee, who knew that if he had to be employed on the terms set by the law in question, he could not be employed at all. This is a predicament that is economic to be sure, but is not without its "human" dimension. Similarly "human" seems the predicament of the appellees in the 1970 case of *Dandridge v. Williams,* who challenged the Maryland Welfare Department's practice of limiting AFDC grants to $250 regardless of family size or need. Yet in language that remains among its favored points of reference, the Court, speaking through Justice Stewart, dismissed the complaint as "social and economic" and therefore essentially Lochneresque.

> [W]e deal with state regulation in the social and economic field, not affecting freedoms guaranteed by the Bill of Rights . . . For this Court to approve the invalidation of state economic or social regulation as "overreaching" would be far too reminiscent of an era when the Court thought the Fourteenth Amendment gave it power to strike down state laws "because they may be unwise, improvident, or out of harmony with a particular school of thought" . . . That era long ago passed into history . . .
>
> To be sure, the cases cited . . . have in the main involved state regulation of business or industry. The administration of public welfare assistance, by contrast, involves the most basic economic needs of impoverished human beings. We recognize the dramatically real factual difference between the cited cases and this one, but we can find no basis for applying a different constitutional standard . . . It is a standard . . . that is true to the principle that the Fourteenth Amendment gives the federal courts no power to impose upon the States their views of wise economic or social policy.

It may be, however—at least it is not the sort of claim one can disprove—that the "right to an abortion," or noneconomic rights generally, accord more closely with "this generation's idealization of America" than the "rights" asserted in either *Lochner* or *Dandridge.* But that attitude, of course, is *precisely* the point of the

Lochner philosophy, which would grant unusual protection to those "rights" that somehow *seem* most pressing, regardless of whether the Constitution suggests any special solicitude for them. The Constitution has little to say about contract, less about abortion, and those who would speculate about which the framers would have been more likely to protect may not be pleased with the answer. The Court continues to disavow the philosophy of *Lochner.* Yet as Justice Stewart's concurrence admits, it is impossible candidly to regard *Roe* as the product of anything else.

That alone should be enough to damn it. Criticism of the *Lochner* philosophy has been virtually universal and will not be rehearsed here. I would, however, like to suggest briefly that although *Lochner* and *Roe* are twins to be sure, they are not identical. While I would hesitate to argue that one is more defensible than the other in terms of judicial style, there *are* differences in that regard that suggest *Roe* may turn out to be the more dangerous precedent.

All the "superimposition of the Court's own value choices" talk is, of course, the characterization of others and not the language of *Lochner* or its progeny. Indeed, those cases did not argue that "liberty of contract" was a preferred constitutional freedom, but rather represented it as merely one among the numerous aspects of "liberty" the Fourteenth Amendment protects, therefore requiring of its inhibitors a "rational" defense.

> In our opinion that section . . . is an invasion of the personal liberty, as well as of the right of property, guaranteed by that Amendment. Such liberty and right embraces the right to make contracts for the purchase of the labor of others and equally the right to make contracts for the sale of one's own labor; each right, however, being subject to the fundamental condition that no contract, whatever its subject matter, can be sustained which the law, upon reasonable grounds, forbids as inconsistent with the public interests or as hurtful to the public order or as detrimental to the common good.

> Undoubtedly, the police power of the State may be exerted to protect purchasers from imposition by sale of short weight loaves . . . Constitutional protection having been invoked, it is the duty of the court to determine whether the challenged provision has reasonable relation to the protection of purchasers of bread against fraud by short weight and really tends to accomplish the purpose for which it was enacted.

Thus the test *Lochner* and its progeny purported to apply is that which would theoretically control the same questions today: whether a plausible argument can be made that the legislative action furthers some permissible government goal. The trouble, of course, is they misapplied it. *Roe*, on the other hand, is quite explicit that the right to an abortion is a "fundamental" one, requiring not merely a "rational" defense for its inhibition but rather a "compelling" one.

A second difference between *Lochner et al.* and *Roe* has to do with the nature of the legislative judgments being second-guessed. In the main, the "refutations" tendered by the *Lochner* series were of two sorts. The first took the form of declarations that the goals in terms of which the legislatures' actions were defended were impermissible. Thus, for example, the equalization of unequal bargaining power and the strengthening of the labor movement are simply ends the legislature had no business pursuing, and consequently its actions cannot thereby be justified. The second form of "refutation" took the form not of denying the legitimacy of the goal relied on but rather of denying the plausibility of the legislature's empirical judgment that its action would *promote* that goal.

> In our judgment it is not possible in fact to discover the connection between the number of hours a baker may work in the bakery and the healthful quality of the bread made by the workman.

> There is no evidence in support of the thought that purchasers have been or are likely to be induced to take a nine and a half or a ten ounce loaf for a pound (16 ounce) loaf, or an eighteen and a half or a 19 ounce loaf for a pound and a half (24 ounce) loaf; and it is contrary to common experience and unreasonable to assume that there could be any danger of such deception.

The *Roe* opinion's "refutation" of the legislative judgment that anti-abortion statutes can be justified in terms of the protection of the fetus takes neither of these forms. The Court grants that protecting the fetus is an "important and legitimate" governmental goal, and of course it does not deny that restricting abortion promotes it. What it does, instead, is simply announce that that goal is not important enough to sustain the restriction. There is little doubt that judgments of this sort were involved in *Lochner et al.*, but what the Court *said* in those cases was not that the legislature had incorrectly balanced two legitimate but competing goals, but rather that the goal it had favored was impermissible or the legislation involved did not really promote it.

Perhaps this is merely a rhetorical difference, but it could prove to be important. *Lochner et al.* were thoroughly disreputable decisions, but at least they did us the favor of sowing the seeds of their own destruction. To say that the equalization of bargaining power or the fostering of the labor movement is a goal outside the ambit of a "police power" broad enough to forbid all contracts the state legislature can reasonably regard "as inconsistent with the public interests or as hurtful to the public order or as detrimental to the common good" is to say something that is, in a word, wrong. And it is just as obviously wrong to declare, for example, that restrictions on long working hours cannot reasonably be said to promote health and safety. *Roe's* "refutation" of the legislative judgment, on the other, is *not* obviously wrong, for the substitution of one nonrational judgment for another concerning the relative importance of a mother's opportunity to live the life she has planned and a fetus's opportunity to live at all, can be labeled neither wrong nor right. The problem with *Roe* is not so much that it bungles the question it sets itself, but rather that it sets itself a question the Constitution has not made the Court's business. It *looks* different from *Lochner*—it has the shape if not the substance of a judgment that is very much the Court's business, one vindicating an interest the Constitution marks as special—and it is for that reason perhaps more dangerous. Of course in a sense it is more candid than *Lochner*. But the employment of a higher standard of judicial review, no matter how candid the recognition that it is indeed higher, loses some of its admirability when it is accompanied by neither a coherent account of why such a standard is appropriate nor any indication of why it has not been satisfied.

V

I do wish "Wolf!" hadn't been cried so often. When I suggest to my students that *Roe* lacks even colorable support in the constitutional text, history, or any other appropriate source of constitutional doctrine, they tell me they've heard all that before. When I point out they haven't heard it before from *me*, I can't really blame them for smiling.

But at least crying "Wolf!" doesn't influence the wolves; crying "Lochner!" may. Of course the Warren Court was aggressive in enforcing its ideals of liberty and equality. *But by and large, it attempted to defend its decisions in terms of inferences from values the Constitution marks as special.* Its inferences were often controversial, but just as often our profession's prominent criticism deigned not to address them on their terms and contented itself with assertions that the Court was indulging in sheer acts of will, ramming its personal preferences down the country's throat—that is was, in a word, Lochnering. One possible judicial response to this style of criticism would be to conclude that one might as well be hanged for a sheep as a goat: So long as you're going to be told, no matter what you say, that all you do is Lochner, you might as well Lochner. Another, perhaps more likely in a new appointee, might be to reason that since Lochnering has so long been standard procedure, "just one more" (in a good cause, of course) can hardly matter. Actual reactions, of course, are not likely to be this self-conscious, but the critical style of offhand dismissal may have taken its toll nonetheless.

Of course the Court has been aware that criticism of much that it has done has been widespread in academic as well as popular circles. But when it looks to the past decade's most prominent academic criticism, it will often find little there to distinguish it from the popular. Disagreements with the chain of inference by which the Court got from the Constitution to its result, if mentioned at all, have tended to be announced in the most conclusory terms, and the impression has often been left that the real quarrel of the Academy, like that of the laity, is with the results the Court has been reaching and perhaps with judicial "activism" in general. Naturally the Court is sensitive to criticism of this sort, but these are issues on which it will, when push comes to shove, trust its own judgment. (And it has no reason not to: Law professors do not agree on what results are "good," and even if they did, there is no reason to assume their judgment is any better on *that* issue than the Court's.) And academic criticism of the sort that might (because it should) have some effect—criticism suggesting misperceptions in the Court's reading of the value structure set forth in the document from which it derives its authority, or unjustifiable inferences it has drawn from that value structure—has seemed for a time somehow out of fashion, the voguish course being simply to dismiss the process by which a disfavored result was reached as Lochnering pure and simple. But if the critics cannot trouble themselves with such details, it is difficult to expect the Court to worry much about them either.

This tendency of commentators to substitute snappy dismissal for careful evaluation of the Court's constitutional inferences—and of course it is simply a tendency, never universally shared and hopefully on the wane—may include among its causes simple laziness, boredom and a natural reluctance to get out of step with the high-steppers. But in part is has also reflected a considered rejection of the view of constitutional adjudication from which my remarks have proceeded. There is a powerful body of opinion that would dismiss the call for substantive criticism—and its underlying assumption that some constitutional inferences are responsible while others are not—as naive. For, the theory goes, except as to the most trivial and least controversial questions (such as the length of a Senator's term), the Constitution speaks in the vaguest and most general terms; the most its clauses can provide are "more or less suitable pegs on which judicial policy choices are hung." Thus anyone who suggests the Constitution can provide significant guidance for today's difficult questions either deludes himself or seeks to delude the Court. Essentially all the Court *can* do is honor the value preferences it sees fit, and it should be graded according to the judgment and skill with which it does so.

One version of this view appears to be held by President Nixon. It is true that in announcing the appointment of Justices Powell and Rehnquist, he described a "judicial conservative"—his kind of Justice—as one who does not "twist or bend the Constitution in order to perpetuate his personal political and social views." But the example he then gave bore witness that he was not so "naive" after all.

> As a judicial conservative, I believe some court decisions have gone too far in the past in weakening the peace forces as against the criminal forces in our society . . . [T] he peace forces must not be denied the legal tools they need to protect the innocent from criminal elements.

That this sort of invitation, to get in there and Lochner for the right goals, can contribute to opinions like *Roe* is obvious. In terms of process, it is just what the President ordered.

The academic version of this general view is considerably more subtle. It agrees that the Court will find little help in the Constitution and therefore has no real choice other than to decide for itself which value preferences to honor, but denies that it should necessarily opt for the preferences favored by the Justices themselves or the President who appointed them. To the extent "progress" is to concern the Justices at all, it should be defined not in terms of what they would like it to be but rather in terms of their best estimate of what over time the American people will make it—that is, they should seek "durable" decisions. This, however, is no easy task, and the goals that receive practically all the critics' attention, and presumably are supposed to receive practically all the Court's, are its own institutional survival and effectiveness.

Whatever the other merits or demerits of this sort of criticism, it plainly is not what it is meant to be—an effective argument for judicial self-restraint. For a Governor Warren or a Senator Black will rightly see no reason to defer to law professors on the probable direction of progress; even less do they need the Academy's advice on what is politically feasible; and they know that despite the Court's history of frequent immersion in hot water, its "institutional position" has been getting stronger for 200 years.

Roe is a case in point. Certainly, many will view it as social progress. (Surely that is the Court's view, and indeed the legislatures had been moving perceptibly, albeit too slowly for many of us, toward relaxing their anti-abortion legislation.) And it is difficult to see how it will weaken the Court's position. Fears of official disobedience are obviously groundless when it is a criminal statute that has been invalidated. To the public the *Roe* decision must look very much like the New York Legislature's recent liberalization of its abortion law. Even in the unlikely event someone should catch the public's ear long enough to charge that the wrong institution did the repealing, they have heard that "legalism" before without taking to the streets. Nor are the political branches, and this of course is what really counts, likely to take up the cry very strenuously: The sighs of relief as this particular albatross was cut from the legislative and executive necks seemed to me audible. Perhaps I heard wrong—I live in the Northeast, indeed not so very far from Hyannis Port. It is even possible that a constitutional amendment will emerge, though that too has happened before without serious impairment of the Position of the Institution. But I doubt one will: *Roe v. Wade* seems like a durable decision.

It is, nevertheless, a very bad decision. Not because it will perceptibly weaken the Court—it won't; and not because it conflicts with either my idea of progress or what the evidence suggests is society's—it doesn't. It is bad because it is bad constitutional law, or rather because it is *not* constitutional law and gives almost no sense of an obligation to try to be.

I am aware the Court cannot simply "lay the Article of the Constitution which is invoked beside the statute which is challenged and . . . decide whether the latter squares with the former." That is precisely the reason commentators are needed.

> [P]recisely because it is the Constitution alone which warrants judicial interference in sovereign operations of the State, the basis of judgment as to the Constitutionality of state action must be a rational one, approaching the text which is the only commission for our power not in a literalistic way, as if we had a tax statute before us, but as the basic charter of our society, setting out in spare but meaningful terms the principles of government.

> No matter how imprecise in application to specific modern fact situations, the constitution guarantees do provide a direction, a goal, an ideal citizen-government relationship. They rule out many alternative directions, goals, and ideals.

And they fail to support the ruling out of others.

Of course that only begins the inquiry. Identification and definition of the values with which the Constitution is concerned will often fall short of indicating with anything resembling clarity the deference to be given those values when the conflict with others society finds important. (Though even here the process is sometimes more helpful than the commentators would allow.) Nor is it often likely to generate, fullblown, the "neutral" principle that will avoid embarrassment in future cases. But though the identification of a constitutional connection is only the beginning of analysis, it is a necessary beginning. The point that often gets lost in the commentary, and obviously got lost in *Roe*, is that *before* the Court can get to the "balancing" stage, *before* it can worry about the next case and the case after that (or even about its institutional position) it is under an obligation to trace its premises to the charter from which it derives its authority. A neutral and durable principle may be a thing of beauty and a joy forever. But if it lacks connection with any value the Constitution marks as special, it is not a constitutional principle and the Court has no business imposing it. I hope that will seem obvious to the point of banality. Yet those of us to whom it does seem obvious have seldom troubled to say so. And because we have not, we must share in the blame for this decision.

Part Two   CIVIL LIBERTIES

CHAPTER 3   "First Amendment Doctrine and the Burger Court"*

THOMAS I. EMERSON**

Though Justice White and Professor Ely find much to fault in *Roe* and *Doe*, the Blackmun opinion actually does not go nearly as far as many supporters as well as many opponents of abortion frequently insinuate. By choosing Justice Blackmun to write the opinion of the Court—a choice Burger made amid much controversy among the brethren since he had originally voted in the minority—the Chief Justice probably headed off a much more sweeping ruling. Had Justice William O. Douglas, for instance, written the opinion, as many believe he should, the result likely would have been painted in much more sharply contrasting hues than was true of the Blackmun product.

The latter opinion, although acknowledging the existence of a "right of personal privacy [which] includes the abortion decision . . .," goes on to say that this right ". . . is not unqualified and must be considered against important state interests in regulation."

In effect, this is a balancing test, a test that the late Justice Felix Frankfurter frequently championed and a test with which the Burger Court seems most comfortable as Professor Thomas I. Emerson points out in the following review of the Court's free speech and free press cases.

*Copyright © 1980, California Law Review, Inc., Reprinted by permission. This article is excerpted and printed without footnotes from the *California Law Review,* Volume 68, pp. 422-481.
**Lines Professor of Law Emeritus, Yale University

In the decade since the Burger Court took over from the Warren Court there has been little change in the position that the system of freedom of expression occupies in our national life. Freedom of expression continues to be accepted as the core of our structure of individual rights. It remains the foundation of our efforts to obtain the proper balance between individual liberty and collective responsibility. And it still provides the framework within which our society tries to achieve necessary, nonviolent, social change.

Throughout this period, political, economic, and social conditions have supported levels of consensus sufficient to maintain the system. Indeed, in some ways political strains on the system have eased as irrational fears of a Communist menace have abated. The material welfare of the country has, at least up to now, continued to expand. And the social climate has not been unduly intolerant or basically hostile to the system. In general, in the last decade the system has not been tested by the strains of crisis conditions.

Nevertheless there have been some significant changes in the system of freedom of expression. These developments have come about in part because of the natural tendency of any vigorous set of legal doctrines to expand to the limits of their logic. In part the developments are due to technological changes in our society, such as those that have resulted in an ever-increasing concentration of the mass media, in the startling growth of data collection and other pressures on our privacy, and in the alarming problems associated with the financing of elections. In part the changes are attributable to the inevitable trend of our society toward collectivism, marked by the dominant role of large organizations, the expansion of governmental functions, and the establishment of vast public and private bureaucracies. Other changing patterns in our complex society have similarly brought forth new issues.

This Article will appraise the effects of the Burger Court's decisions on the system of freedom of expression. It will undertake to demonstrate that because of the Court's predilection for ad hoc balancing, its failure to take proper account of the dynamics of suppression, and its unwillingness to develop innovative doctrines in response to changing needs, the system has become less effective at serving its underlying values. Part I will survey developments in the fundamental structure of the system over the past decade. Part II will examine various commentators' proposals for the improvement of basic first amendment doctrine. Against this background, Part III will analyze the application of first amendment doctrine by the Burger Court in the various cases that have come before it. Finally, Part IV will evaluate general theoretical approaches to first amendment doctrine.

DEVELOPMENTS IN THE BASIC STRUCTURE OF THE SYSTEM OF FREEDOM OF EXPRESSION

The basic structure of the system of freedom of expression, so far as its legal features are concerned, is comprised of three major elements. At its root are the fundamental values that the system is intended to serve. Next are the primary instumentalities charged with maintaining the system: law and legal institutions. Finally, the system must include some recognition of the practical problems—the "dynamics"—involved in the actual operation of the system. This recognition must, of course, be made primarily in the courts when they seek to apply the law to particular problems. Developments in these three areas during the last decade establish the context in which the doctrinal work of the Burger Court must be judged.

A. Underlying Values

In previous writings I have attempted to group the traditional values underlying the system of freedom of expression into four categories. Over the years, we have come to view freedom of expression as essential to: (1) individual self-fulfillment; (2) the advance of knowledge and the discovery of truth; (3) participation in decisionmaking by all members of society; and (4) maintenance of the proper balance between stability and change.

These values must be considered not in isolation, but as an integrated set. Each is necessary, but not in itself sufficient, for the four of them are interdependent. Thus, a system designed to serve only the interest in orderly change could not succeed in the long run; in a democratic society such change can only be effected through active participation by the policy in decisionmaking. Furthermore, such participation would not be possible without a systemic commitment to the advance of knowledge or the discovery of truth.

It should be remembered, also, that this set of values does not automatically translate into first amendment legal doctrine. The contribution of the law and legal institutions to their achievement can only take place if specific legal rules are formulated to implement the underlying value structure. But that structure does establish the goals we seek, guide the process of creating legal rules, and provide a standard by which the success of those rules can be tested.

During the past decade we have continued to accept the traditional set of values outlined above as the fundamental basis upon which our system of freedom of expression rests. Although variations have been suggested, no major changes have been proposed or new values added. There has, however, been considerable discussion, and some elaboration, of the four categories. Most of those who have commented on these matters have been concerned with one specific value, rather than with the whole set. In this respect, particularly because of what they omit, their positions do not conform to that set out above. Nevertheless, the discussion has contributed to our understanding of the value structure.

• • • • • •

APPLICATION OF FIRST AMENDMENT DOCTRINE BY THE BURGER COURT

The Burger Court inherited a mixed legacy from the Warren Court. In general, the Warren Court protected expression to an unprecedented degree. However, this resulted more from a strongly favorable attitude toward first amendment values than from a well-developed theory of the first amendment. As a result, the Warren Court's decisions contained numerous ambiguities, loopholes, and loosely formulated rules. Moreover, decisions supporting first amendment claims frequently rested on grounds unrelated to the first amendment. The Burger Court has displayed far less sensitivity to first amendment values than did the Warren Court. On the whole it has refused to press first amendment doctrine forward but rather has tended to withdraw, frequently by taking advantage of openings in Warren Court decisions. The lack of a coherent theory has persisted.

A. The Fundamental Approach

The Burger Court has fully accepted the traditional set of values underlying the first amendment. It does not often articulate those values, however, and it does not always take them to their logical conclusion. For example, it has not been responsive to the call for development of the self-fulfullment value, as witnessed by its treatment of the long-hair cases. Nor has it been willing to carry the citizen participation value to the point of granting additional access to the facilities for communication. On the other hand, the Court has definitely rejected suggestions that the scope of the first amendment be limited to narrow categories such as "political speech."

The Burger Court has also adhered to the traditional position that racist and totalitarian expression are entitled to the protection of the first amendment. These issues were dramatically presented in the *Skokie* case. When a small band of Nazis announced their intention to march in full regalia through the Chicago suburb of Skokie, a village that was the residence of a large number of survivors of the German concentration camps, the village authorities took a series of measures to prevent them. The controversy reached the Supreme Court only on procedural issues and the Court did not have occasion to address the question in detail. But it did make clear that the conduct involved "rights protected by the First Amendment."

Two other issues of fundamental doctrine deserve more extended discussion. One is the Burger Court's treatment of the "preferred position" doctrine. The other is the question of what conduct is entitled to the special protection of the first amendment.

1. Preferred Position

As already noted, the core of first amendment doctrine is that certain conduct, roughly designated "expression," occupies a "preferred position" in our constitutional system. The Warren Court vigorously supported this concept. It was, indeed, at the root of that Court's sympathetic approach toward first amendment rights. The Burger Court has not repudiated the preferred position doctrine. But is has never seemed to accept it wholeheartedly and has frequently ignored it.

Examples of the Burger Court's attitude are numerous. In *California v. LaRue,* for instance, the Court dealt with regulations that prohibited certain kinds of entertainment in bars or nightclubs where liquor was served. It conceded that some of the conduct thus proscribed was not obscene, and hence constituted expression within the purview of the first amendment. A majority of the Court, however, upheld the regulation on the ground that the State's conclusion that the regulation was useful in preventing illegal conduct in bars and nightclubs was not "unreasonable" or "irrational."

A similar approach guided the Court in *Young v. American Mini Theatres, Inc.* There a Detroit zoning ordinance imposed severe restrictions upon the location of motion picture theatres that exhibited sexually explicit "adult" films. The Court agreed that the films in question were not obscene and hence were expression of a type that the first amendment was intended to protect. Nevertheless, a majority of the Court upheld the ordinance. Four Justices rested the case on the proposition that "the city's interest in attempting to preserve the quality of urban life is one that must be accorded high respect," and that "the city must be allowed a reasonable opportunity to experiment with solutions to admittedly serious problems." Justice Powell concurred in the decision, saying that there was no "reason to question that the degree of incidental encroachment upon . . . expression was the minimum necessary to further the purpose of the ordinance."

The Burger Court's neglect of the preferred position doctrine is manifest in other cases as well. In *Lehman v. City of Shaker Heights,* the Court was faced with a regulation which, although it allowed the sale of commercial advertising space in the cars of the municipal rapid transit system, prohibited the sale of the same space for political advertisements. A majority of the Court rejected the first amendment challenge. The plurality opinion of four Justices framed the question as simply whether the policy was "arbitrary, capricious, or invidious," and concluded that the city had advanced "reasonable legislative objectives." In short, the Burger Court betrayed a preference for legislative judgment over first amendment values.

A somewhat different aspect of the preferred position concept arose in *Mount Healthy City School District v. Doyle.* In this case, a school board refused to rehire a teacher because he had engaged in activities that were found to be only partially protected by the first amendment. The district court found that the protected expression had played a "substantial part" in the school board's decision, and ordered the teacher reinstated. The Supreme Court remanded the case to the district court to determine whether the board might have reached the same result if it had not taken into consideration the conduct protected by the first amendment.

Similarly, in *Houchins v. KQED, Inc.,* the Court refused to find that the public or the press had any first amendment right to obtain access to a county jail. And in *Gannett Co. v. De Pasquale,* the Court held that a trial judge could exclude the public and the press from any criminal pretrial proceeding when he found that their presence would pose a "reasonable probability of prejudice" to the defendant. In these cases, as well as in *Mount Healthy,* the Court scarcely displayed a serious effort to give freedom of expression a preferred position.

All of these cases, and others, suggest that where the Burger Court does not favor the type of expression involved, where it feels inclined to defer to legislative judgment, or where it prefers another social interest, it does not feel bound by the preferred position doctrine. Its failure to start its analysis in freedom of expression cases from this doctrinal base is likely to lead the Court to conclusions that give little effort to first amendment values.

2. *Conduct Covered by the First Amendment*

The Burger Court, like the Warren Court, has rejected all rigorous definitional approaches to the question of what conduct is to be covered by the first amendment, including the "expression-action" approach. It cannot, of course, avoid the question; analysis of a first amendment issue must begin by determining whether the first amendment applies at all. The Burger Court's approach, in essence, has been to hold that some conduct of a purely verbal nature is outside the purview of the first amendment altogether, that otherwise all conduct having an "expressive" or "communicative" element is covered, and that some kinds of covered conduct are more "pure speech" than others. All of these doctrines were inherited from the Warren Court.

The exclusion of certain conduct that is unquestionably "expression" derives from the famous dictum in *Chaplinsky v. New Hampshire*:

There are certain well-defined and narrowly limited classes of speech, the prevention and punishment of which have never been thought to raise any Constitutional problem. These include the lewd and obscene, the profane, the libelous, and the insulting or "fighting" words—those which by their very utterance inflict injury or tend to incite an immediate breach of the peace. It has been well observed that such utterances are no essential part of any exposition of ideas, and are of such slight social value as a step to truth that any benefit that may be derived from them is clearly outweighed by the social interest in order and morality.

The *Chaplinsky* dictum, although frequently quoted, is totally incompatible with modern first amendment theory. It makes the exclusions turn on whether the expression has "social value as a step to truth." One of the cardinal principles of first amendment doctrine, however, is that the government may not base any restriction upon its determination that the content of expression is good or bad, or that it has "social value" or does not.

Because of this blatant conflict, there has been some tendency for the Supreme Court to move away from the *Chaplinsky* doctrine. Thus, in *New York Times Co. v. Sullivan* the Warren Court removed libel from the *Chaplinsky* list, and in *Cohen v. California* the Burger Court in effect took "profane" off the list. On the whole, however, that doctrine remains alive. The Burger Court still treats obscenity as expression outside first amendment coverage. Indeed, it has compounded the *Chaplinsky* error by rejecting the Warren Court's determination that, in order to be "obscene," materials must be "utterly without redeeming social importance." It has instead substituted the less demanding requirement that the material "lacks serious literary, artistic, political, or scientific value." And the "fighting words" exclusion still remains, although the Burger Court has tended less to provide an automatic exclusion from coverage than to determine whether the words would incite to imminent lawless action.

Apart from the *Chaplinsky* exclusions, the Burger Court continues to follow the position taken in *United States v. O'Brien*, where the Warren Court held that any "communicative element" in conduct "is sufficient to bring into play the First Amendment." Thus, in *Spence v. Washington* the Court found that a college student's display of an American flag, upside down and with a peace symbol attached, was conduct "sufficiently imbued with elements of communication to fall within the scope of the First and Fourteenth Amendments."

At the same time, however, the Burger Court continues the Warren Court's distinction between "pure speech" and other speech. In *Landmark Communications, Inc. v. Virginia,* dealing with a Virginia statute that prohibited the publication of information concerning the confidential proceedings of the State's Judicial Inquiry Commission, the Court made a point of the fact that the newspaper involved was engaged in conduct that "lies near the core of the First Amendment." Like the Warren Court, the Burger Court has never enunciated any specific standard for determining the method by which first amendment "core" expression should be protected as compared with other expression.

In sum, the Burger Court's approach to determining the coverage of the first amendment has led to ill-considered exclusions and a generally imprecise definition of that coverage. The *Chaplinsky* exclusions are not related to the functions of the system of freedom of expression. And the concepts of "communicative elements" and "pure speech" are useful only in connection with vague balancing tests.

B. Major Doctrines

The question of the appropriate degree of protection for conduct covered by the first amendment has been the primary focus of attention for the Burger Court. With the exception of Justices Black and Douglas, the Warren Court did not accept the full protection doctrine and the Burger Court has not departed from this position. Indeed, the loose definition of expression as "communicative" conduct makes full protection or any doctrine approaching it unworkable. Nor does the Burger Court take the position that expression is presumptively protected unless it falls within some narrowly defined exception. Its main tools for according protection to conduct falling within the ambit of the first amendment are the doctrines of clear and present danger (or some variant), balancing, and prior restraint.

1. Clear and Present Danger

In cases involving militant or radical speech that, it is feared, may result in some violation of law, the Burger Court utilizes the *Brandenburg* version of the clear and present danger test. The *Brandenburg* case itself dealt with the speech of a Ku Klux Klan leader who urged a march on Washington to take "revengeance" upon the President, Congress, and the Supreme Court. The Supreme Court, in a per curiam opinion, reversed a conviction under the Ohio Criminal Syndicalism Act, stating that "the constitutional guarantees of free speech and free press do not permit a State to forbid or proscribe advocacy of the use of force or of law violation except where such advocacy is directed to inciting or producing imminent lawless action and is likely to incite or produce such action." As noted above, the test is a combination of the original clear and present danger test, which looked to the potential effect of the speech, and an "incitement" test, which looked to the content of the speech.

The Burger Court reaffirmed the *Brandenburg* test in *Hess v. Indiana*, again in a per curiam opinion, when it reversed a conviction based upon a statement by a leader of a college antiwar demonstration that "We'll take the fucking street later (or again)." The Court has also employed the test in cases where militant advocacy was not being punished directly but was being used as a disqualification for some government benefit or privilege. Thus, in *Healy v. James* the Court ruled that a state college could not refuse official recognition to a chapter of the Students for a Democratic Society on the ground that its advocacy would be "disruptive" unless the advocacy met the *Brandenburg* standard. And in *Communist Party of Indiana v. Whitcomb* it applied the *Brandenburg* test to invalidate an Indiana statute that excluded from the ballot any party that would not take an oath that it did not "advocate the overthrow of local, state or national government by force or violence."

The original clear and present danger test was employed by the Warren Court in *Wood v. Georgia* and earlier decisions in contempt of court cases, where the expression sought to be punished consisted of vigorous criticism of a court or its personnel. The Burger Court has cited *Wood v. Georgia* with approval and would presumably follow it in a similar situation. Beyond this, however, the Burger Court's use of the clear and present danger test has been erratic and confusing.

In *Nebraska Press Association v. Stuart*, the Burger Court considered the validity of a restraining order issued by a trial judge in a criminal case enjoining the local media from publishing information about the case that would implicate the accused. The Court, speaking through Chief Justice Burger, resurrected the Hand-Vinson version of the clear and present danger test taken from *Dennis v. United States*, namely, "whether the gravity of the 'evil,' discounted by its improbability, justifies such invasion of free speech as is necessary to avoid the danger." This variation of the clear and present danger test had not been utilized by the Supreme Court since its creation in the *Dennis* case and had been thought to be long dead. Moreover, in applying the test, Chief Justice Burger treated it as a balancing test, including in it a "least drastic means" element:

> To ... [apply the test], we must examine the evidence before the trial judge when the order was entered to determine (a) the nature and extent of pretrial news coverage; (b) whether other measures would be likely to mitigate the effects of unrestrained pretrial publicity; and (c) how effectively a restraining order would operate to prevent the threatened danger. The precise terms of the restraining order are also important. We must then consider whether the record supports the entry of a prior restraint on publication, one of most extraordinary remedies known to our jurisprudence.

The Burger Court also discussed the clear and present danger test in *Landmark Communications, Inc. v. Virginia*, mentioned above, a case also involving the administration of justice. Chief Justice Burger, writing for six members of the

Court, noted that the Supreme Court of Virginia had relied upon the clear and present danger test in rejecting the first amendment claim and stated, "We question the relevance of that standard here." The Court went on, however, to apply the test:

> [W]e cannot accept the mechanical application of the test which led that court to its conclusion . . . Properly applied, the test requires a court to make its own inquiry into the imminence and magnitude of the danger said to flow from the particular utterance and then to balance the character of the evil, as well as its likelihood, against the need for free and unfettered expression. The possibility that other measures will serve the State's interest should also be weighed.

In sum, the Burger Court employs the clear and present danger test only in limited situations. It is used, in its *Brandenburg* form, in cases concerned with advocacy of illegal action. In cases involving the administration of criminal justice it may or may not be utilized. In other areas it has not been invoked. Moreover, except possibly in its *Brandenburg* form, the clear and present danger test has become, in the hands of the Burger Court, pure balancing. Those who hoped for a wider application of the clear and present danger test, or for its use in a "categorical" form, have been disappointed.

2. Balancing

The primary test employed by the Burger Court to determine the scope of first amendment protection is balancing. Indeed, as the number of advocacy cases has declined, the balancing test has come to represent the routine approach of the Burger Court to first amendment issues. The test has not always been applied in the same way, however, and occasionally it is not used at all.

a. Where the Burger Court Has Used Balancing

The balancing test has been utilized by the Burger Court in all types of cases. It has frequently been applied where the government restriction takes the form of a direct prohibition or regulation of expression. Thus it has become the standard test in cases dealing with such matters as the publication of information the government wishes to keep confidential, flag desecration laws, offensive speech, defamation, and limitations on expression in connection with political campaigns. The balancing test is also invoked in cases involving indirect restrictions on expression, where the regulation is ostensibly aimed at some other conduct but has a substantial impact upon expression, as in the *American Mini Theatres* case. It is also applied to situations where special factors call for unconventional rules, as in cases concerned with the rights of government employees or the right of the press to gather news.

The balancing test is used whether the opposing interest involved is a constitutional right or a nonconstitutional interest. It may function either as an ad hoc test to decide a particular case or as the basis for developing a more general rule.

What is remarkable about the Burger Court's use of the balancing test is that it is employed even in what appear to be the most obvious cases for upholding the first amendment claim. Thus, in *Landmark Communications, Inc. v. Virginia,* mentioned above, the Virginia statute in effect established a miniature "official secrets act" that would have imposed a criminal penalty for the publication of any information originating in a proceeding before the Judicial Inquiry Commission, no matter how the information had been obtained and no matter how many others had already published it. It would be hard to find a more blatant violation of the first amendment. Nevertheless, the Court carefully balanced the interests on each side. Similarly, in *Wooley v. Maynard,* the Court dealt with a New Hampshire statute that made it a crime to obscure the words "Live Free or Die" on state license plates. The defendants in the case were Jehovah's Witnesses who considered the motto repugnant to their moral, religious, and political beliefs. The issue would seem to be a clearcut one of the government forcing unwilling citizens to make an affirmation of belief, a practice long since forbidden by *West Virginia State Board of Education v. Barnette,* the flag salute case. Yet the Court felt it necessary to weigh the State's "countervailing interest" to see if it justified the invasion of the right to hold a belief.

Occasionally, however, the Burger Court has declined to use balancing. In *Miami Herald Publishing Co. v. Tornillo,* the Court was confronted with a Florida statute that required newspapers to publish a reply whenever a political candidate had been attacked in its columns. It unanimously struck down the statute, but did not use balancing language. Rather, as the Warren Court had done in *New York Times Co. v. Sullivan,* the Burger Court examined the impact of the regulation upon the journalistic process and found that it imposed a substantial burden. In *Linmark Associates v. Willingboro,* the Court dealt with a town ordinance, directed at panic selling and white flight to the suburbs, that prohibited the posting of "For Sale" signs on real estate. In another unanimous decision, it held the ordinance invalid. The decision rested in part on balancing doctrine, but was primarily based on what appeared to be a brand of full protection. The town council, said the Court, "has sought to restrict the free flow of these data because it fears that otherwise homeowners will make decisions inimical to what the Council views as the homeowner's self-interest and the corporate interest of the township."

b. Variation in the Balancing Process

The manner in which the Burger Court strikes the balance between first amendment claims and other interests has varied widely from case to case. In the form of balancing most favorable to first amendment values, the Burger Court has subjected opposing interests to "exacting scrutiny." For example, in *Buckley v. Valeo,* where the Court was concerned with limitations on contributions and expenditures in political campaigns, it spelled out the exacting scrutiny standard to require that (1) the government demonstrate (2) "a sufficiently important interest," and (3) employ "means closely drawn to avoid unnecessary abridgement" of first amendment freedoms. Similarly, in *First National Bank of Boston v. Belotti,* striking down a statute that forbade corporations to make contributions or expenditures in order to influence the vote in a referendum, the Court again applied the "exacting scrutiny" standard, declaring that (1) "the burden is on the Government to show" (2) "a subordinating interest which is compelling," and (3) to employ "means closely drawn." The third requirement has been phrased as a straight "less drastic means" test. Although the Court has never clearly stated the circumstances under which it will invoke strict scrutiny balancing, this version of the balancing test appears most frequently in cases involving either "political speech" or prior restraints.

At times the Court has tilted the balance less sharply in the direction of the first amendment. For example, in *Wooley v. Maynard,* the Court looked into whether "the State's countervailing interest is sufficiently compelling."

In some decisions, the weighing process has appeared basically neutral; neither the first amendment interests nor the opposing government interests enjoyed any presumption. In *Landmark Communications,* for instance, the Court simply sought to ascertain whether the State's interests were "sufficient to justify the encroachment on first amendment guarantees." In *Gertz,* it attempted to find an "accommodation" between the interests involved. And in *Gannett Co. v. DePasquale,* it upheld the exclusion of the public and the press from a pretrial hearing " on an assessment of the competing societal interests involved."

Ironically, the form of balancing that gives the least protection to first amendment rights was first enunciated by the Warren Court. In *United States v. O'Brien,* that Court held that the government restriction—a prohibition against draft card burning—was valid if (1) "it furthers an important or substantial governmental interest," (2) the governmental interest is "unrelated to the suppression of free expressions," and (3) "the incidental restriction on alleged first amendment freedoms is no greater than is essential to the furtherance of that interest." The *O'Brien* test is hardly balancing at all. Once the government finds a way to direct its regulation at some conduct other than expression itself—not a difficult task— then it need merely show that the restriction is no greater than is necessary to further the nonexpression interest. Unless this last requirement is applied as a rigorous "less drastic means" test, which *O'Brien* does not contemplate, there is virtually no likelihood that the balance will be struck in favor of first amendment values.

The Burger Court, in effect although not explicitly, applied the *O'Brien* test in *Young v. American Mini Theatres, Inc.,* the Detroit zoning case. The plurality opinion of four Justices, written by Justice Stevens, treated the regulation as primarily a zone ordinance, directed at improving residential neighborhoods and only incidentally affecting expression. It then balanced merely to the extent of finding that the "record disclosed a factual basis" for the government's decision. Justice Powell, concurring, expressly applied the *O'Brien* test.

c. A Critique of Balancing

The Burger Court's use of the balancing test demonstrates the validity of the objections that consistently have been made to this free-wheeling approach to protection of freedom of expression. In nearly every case, the Justices could have struck the balance in favor of either side, and in most cases there was disagreement with the balance that prevailed. *Elrod v. Burns, Bellotti,* and *Herbert v. Lando* are ready examples. Furthermore, the Burger Court has made no progress in refining the test by delineating the weight to be given to specific factors. Rather, it has devised a number of variations and has applied them erratically. Equally important, however, is the fact that uninhibited use of the balancing test has led the Burger Court into other positions that are in basic conflict with traditional first amendment theory.

i. Measuring the value of expression. The Burger Court has come more and more to weigh in the balance its view of the social value of the expression being challenged. Thus in *American Mini Theatres,* the four Justices subscribing to the plurality opinion expressly took the position that "the stated principle that there may be no restriction whatever on expressive activity because of its content" must be "sometimes qualified." Pursuant to this position the plurality declared that "there is surely a less vital interest in the uninhibited exhibition of material that is on the borderline between pornography and artistic expression than in the free dissemination of ideas of social and political significance." It went on to hold that "society's interest in protecting this type of expression is of a wholly different, and lesser, magnitude than the interest in untrammeled political debate." The attitude of the four Justices toward first amendment theory became manifest when the opinion concluded:

Whether political oratory or philosophical discussion moves us to applaud or to despise what is said, every schoolchild can understand why our duty to defend the right to speak remains the same. But few of us would march our sons and daughters off to war to preserve the citizen's right to see "Specified Sexual Activities" exhibited in the theaters of our choice. Even though the First Amendment protects communication in this area from total suppression, we hold that the State may legitimately use the content of these materials as the basis for placing them in a different classification from other motion pictures.

In *Federal Communications Commission v. Pacifica Foundation*, three of the same Justices formed a plurality that held that the FCC could validly impose sanctions upon a radio station for broadcasting a program entitled "Filthy Words," even though the program was not obscene and hence should have been protected by the first amendment. Again arguing that the rule that "prohibits all governmental regulation that depends on the content of speech" is not "absolute," the Justices found that "offensive" words occupied a low place "in the hierarchy of First Amendment values."

Thus the Burger Court is only one vote shy of a majority that expressly takes into account its view of the social value of a particular communication in determing whether or to what extent such expression will be protected under the first amendment. Further, that approach is implicit in other rulings subscribed to by a clear majority of the Court. For example, in refusing to extend the "actual malice" rule to situations where a "private individual" rather than a "public official" or "public figure" claims to have been libeled, the Court incorporated into its balance the proposition that "there is no constitutional value in false statements of fact," quoting *Chaplinsky* to the effect that such utterances "are of such slight social value as a step to truth that any benefit that may be derived from them is clearly outweighed by the social interest in order and morality." Similarly, in limiting the "exacting scrutiny" standard largely to cases involving "political speech," on the ground that such expression "is at the heart of the First Amendment's protection," the Court is clearly making a judgment as to the social value of the expression involved. The same is true in commercial speech cases where, unlike other forms of expression, "deceptive and misleading" communications can be controlled by the government.

These moves in the direction of weighing the social value of the particular expression for which first amendment protection is sought inevitably follow from the expanding use of the balancing process. It is very difficult, perhaps impossible, to calculate the social interest in a particular communication without explicitly or implicitly taking into consideration the social value that the balancer attaches to that expression. Yet, under longstanding first amendment theory, this is a judgment the government is not entitled to make. As the Supreme Court said many years ago, "Wholly neutral futilities, of course, come under the protection of free speech as fully as do Keats' poems or Donne's sermons."

ii. Measuring the degree of impairment. Another aspect of the balancing test is that it considers the degree of infringement on first amendment rights and denies protection where the impact of the government regulation, although substantial, is not deemed sufficient. Thus in *Gannett Co. v. DePasquale,* the Court approved denial of access to a pretrial hearing in part on the ground that the denial "was not absolute but only temporary." Likewise in *Zurcher v. Stanford Daily* the Court, balancing the impact of a search warrant rather than a subpoena in obtaining evidence from newspaper files, concluded that "[w]hatever incremental effect there may be in this regard . . . it does not make a constitutional difference in our judgment." In *American Mini Theatres,* again, the plurality of the Court was "not persuaded" that the Detroit ordinance prohibiting movie theaters from operating in designated areas had "a significant deterrent effect on the exhibition of films protected by the First Amendment." And in his concurrence Justice Powell down-graded the weight of the first amendment interest by calling the impact "incidental and minimal." In *Elrod v. Burns,* three Justices, voting to uphold a patronage system that resulted in the dismissal of governmental employees because of their political affiliation, characterized the impact as a "relatively modest intrusion on First Amendment interests."

It has always been a basic tenet of first amendment doctrine that any sub-stantial abridgement of first amendment rights—any significant chilling effect—is sufficient to trigger the protection of that constitutional guarantee. The balancing test, particularly as employed by the Burger Court, is chipping away at this basic principle and is thus contributing further to the erosion of freedom of expression's preferred position.

iii. Less restrictive alternatives. A third consequence of the balancing test is that it draws into the balance the question whether alternative means of communi-cation are open to those whose expression is being restricted. Traditional first amendment doctrine has long held that the existence of other channels of com-munication cannot be used as a justification for the government to close off the particular means of expression that the speaker or listener has chosen. Until recent-ly the Burger Court has adhered to this doctrine. In the *Pacifica* case, however, a majority of the Court took another tack. The three adherents to the plurality opinion argued that "adults who feel the need may purchase tapes and records or go to theatres and nightclubs to hear these words." And the two Justices who joined to make a majority were even more emphatic: "The Commission's holding does not prevent willing adults from purchasing Carlin's record, from attending his performances, or, indeed, from reading the transcript reprinted as an appendix to the Court's opinion." Here again the balancing test is beginning to undermine hitherto firm first amendment doctrine.

3. Prior Restraint

The doctrine forbidding prior restraint is one of the major underpinnings of the system of freedom of expression. Its roots go back to the English censorship laws against which John Milton protested. It is one of the few principles clearly incorporated in the first amendment by the drafters. And it has been widely accepted as serving a vital function in maintaining the right to freedom of expression. The doctrine holds that the government may not, through a system of censorship, by use of a court injunction, or otherwise, prohibit or restrict expression in advance of publication, even though the material published may be subject to subsequent punishment. The rationale of the doctrine lies in the fact that, taken as a whole, a system of prior restraint is likely to be far more restrictive of expression than subsequent punishment, at least in the absence of a police state.

The prohibition against prior restraints has always been suject to certain exception. In the case that first established the docrine, *Near v. Minnesota*, Chief Justice Hughes stated that the rule "is not absolutely unlimited," but that limitations would be found "only in exceptional cases." The Warren Court, in *Times Film Corp. v. City of Chicago*, made an exception for motion picture censorship boards established to screen out "obscene" films. Licensing systems for allocation of scarce physical facilities have also been upheld. Until recently, however, these exceptions had remained restricted to narrowly drawn categories, and, on the whole, were capable of relatively precise application.

a. Ad Hoc Balancing in Prior Restraint Cases

The Burger Court has recognized the significance of the doctrine of prior restraint and has in fact never sustained a prior restraint that did not fall within one of the specific exceptions just noted. Its handling of prior restraint cases has, however, deprived the exceptions of their categorical nature and has left the prior restraint rule seriously weakened.

The prior restraint doctrine confronted a major challenge in *New York Times Co. v. United States,* the Pentagon Papers case, during the early days of the Burger Court. The government had sought an injunction against the New York Times, the Washington Post, and other newspapers to restrain the publication of the Pentagon Papers on the ground that publication would cause "grave and irreparable injury" to the United States. In a six to three vote, accompanied by a per curiam opinion, the Court denied the government's request, saying that it had not met the "heavy burden" of justifying a prior restraint. The more precise positions of the individual Justices were set forth in nine separate opinions. Justices Black and Douglas held to their full protection view: the government possessed no constitutional power to "make laws enjoining publication of current news and abridging freedom of the press in the name of 'national security.' " Justice Brennan took a similar stance but would have allowed an exception in the area of tactical military operations: "only governmental allegation and proof that publication must inevitably, directly and immediately cause the occurrence of an event kindred to imperiling the safety of a transport already at sea can support even the issuance of an interim restraining order." Justices Stewart and White, recognizing the "concededly extraordinary protection against prior restraints," nevertheless were willing to allow an injunction upon a showing of "direct, immediate, and irreparable damage to our Nation or its people." Justice Marshall did not reach first amendment issues. Chief Justice Burger and Justices Harlan and Blackmun, dissenting, felt that the courts should exercise only an extremely limited review where the executive had determined that disclosure "would irreparably impair the national security."

The Burger Court has not had occasion to rule again on the doctrine of prior restaint in a national security case. It seems a fair assumption from the Pentagon Papers case, however, that it would not impose any stricter barrier to prior restraint than the requirement of a showing of "direct, immediate, and irreparable damage," as urged by Justices Stewart and White.

The other major decision in which the Burger Court has considered the doctrine of prior restraint is *Nebraska Press Association v. Stuart*. As noted above, that case dealt with a trial court judge's order restraining the local news media from publishing information about the accused in a pending murder case. Chief Justice Berger, in an opinion with which four other Justices concurred, reviewed earlier prior restraint cases and concluded that "[t]he thread running through all these cases is that prior restraints on speech and publication are the most serious and least tolerable infringement on First Amendment rights." He refused to hold, however, that the "barriers to prior restraint" were "absolute" in a fair trial case. Instead, he applied the Hand-Vinson variation of the clear and present danger test, ending up with elaborate ad hoc balancing. The conditions laid down by Chief Justice Burger for upholding a prior restraint in a fair trial case are hard to meet, but the facts and circumstances must be examined in each case. Justice Brennan, joined by Justices Stewart and Marshall, adopted an absolute position. They stated that "resort to prior restraints on the freedom of the press is a constitutionally impermissible method for enforcing" the right to a fair trial. Justice Stevens refrained from fully committing himself to Justice Brennan's view, but was inclined to agree with him.

One further case, involving less portentous issues, illustrates the manner in which the Burger Court has dealt with prior restraint questions. In *Organization for a Better Austin v. Keefe,* a real estate broker obtained an injuction restraining a neighborhood organization from distributing leaflets criticizing his "blockbusting" tactics, on the grounds that the organization's activities invaded his privacy and caused him irreparable damage. The Supreme Court labelled the injunction a prior restraint and reversed. Again it balanced, saying the proponent of the injunction "carries a heavy burden of showing justification for the imposition of such a restraint," and concluded that he had "not met that burden" in this case.

It is clear from these decisions that the Burger Court does not view the prior restraint doctrine as a prohibition on all prior restraints subject to certain categorical exceptions such as obscene motion pictures or communications about tactical military operations. Rather, in its view, the doctrine simply creates a "presumption" against the validity of the restraint and thereby imposes a "heavy burden" on the government to justify the particular restriction then before the Court.

b. The Doctrinal Effects

The Burger Court's approach to prior restraints reduces the force of the doctrine in two ways. First, the requirement of ad hoc scrutiny of prior restraints is itself likely to result in a "de facto" prior restraint. For example, in a national security case, the government needs only to file a complaint alleging that publication of certain information will cause "direct, immediate, and irreparable" harm to national security. The court will then issue an order restraining publication to allow the government to present its case. Hearings and appeals will follow. Justice Brennan pointed out the consequences of this procedure in the Pentagon Papers case:

[I] f the Executive Branch seeks judicial aid in preventing publication, it must inevitably submit the basis upon which that aid is sought to scrutiny by the judiciary. And therefore, every restraint issued in this case, whatever its form, has violated the First Amendment—and not less so because that restraint was justified as necessary to afford the courts an opportunity to examine the claim more thoroughly.

This is exactly what happened when the government sought to enjoin *The Progressive* magazine from publishing an article on the manufacture of the hydrogen bomb. The Supreme Court refused to order an expedited appeal from the district court injunction against publication. Although the case was ultimately dismissed by the court of appeals, *The Progressive* remained under effective prior restraint for nearly seven months.

Second, and equally important, the Burger Court's approach affords little guidance to the lower courts. In a fair trial case, for instance, the trial judge must weigh various imponderables in each case. Some of these may be mere speculations about future events. The tendency of a trial judge in such a situation is to avoid the risks of prejudicial publicity through the sacrifice of first amendment interests.

In short, unless the prior restraint doctrine is formulated as an absolute prohibition, with possible exceptions stated in precise categorical terms, it is of limited value in maintaining a system of freedom of expression. The Burger Court has rejected such a formulation and has, in effect, made the prior restraint doctrine into an ad hoc balancing test.

• • • • • •

CONCLUSION

Broad agreement concerning the basic values that underlie our system of freedom of expression continues to exist. Unfortunately, the quest for effective legal doctrine that would translate those values into reality has not been successful. Commentators have not been able to devise sufficiently disciplined rules to control the forces and institutions that impair the functioning of the system. Nor has the Burger Court. The general approach of that Court was epitomized by Justice Blackmun in *Bigelow v. Virginia,* when he wrote for the majority: "Advertising, like all public expression, may be subject to reasonable regulation that serves a legitimate public interest." The outcome has been that freedom of expression has by no means received the special protection to which it is theoretically entitled. Rather, it has been given only a watered-down due process protection. A more rigorous doctrinal framework is imperative if the system is to survive the stresses that are likely to come.

CHAPTER 4   "The Irrelevance of the Constitution:
The Religion Clauses of the First
Amendment and the Supreme Court"*

PHILIP B. KURLAND**

Perhaps the commentary or criticism that is most often heard of
the Burger Court is that it seems unwilling or unable to base its decisions on anything approaching clearly defined constitutional principles.
Surely this was a theme that ran throughout the previous article by
Professor Emerson and it is echoed equally loudly in this selection from
the writings of Professor Philip Kurland.

Kurland is an acknowledged authority on church-state questions,
one of the more vexing areas of constitutional law. But why is this area
so troublesome? Why, more particularly, is it so controversial and why
has it recently become one of the focal points for criticism of the
Court?

Part of the answer to this series of questions may be found in the
fact that the Court, and here we speak both of the Warren and Burger
Courts, by failing to ground its decisions on something akin to what
Professor Herbert Wechsler called "general, neutral principles of constitutional law," has conveyed the clear impression that court decisions in this area are matters of personal preference and not of constitutional right.

If this is all they are, or if this is what they are perceived to be,
it is no surprise that advocates of aid to parochial schools and proponents of prayer in the public school refuse to give up their battle
despite repeated defeats in the courts.

---

*Reprinted with permission from *Villanova Law Review*, Volume 24, No. 1, pp. 3-27. ©
Copyright 1978 by Villanova University. The article is excerpted and printed without foot-
notes.
**Professor of Law, University of Chicago Law School

• • • • • •

The thesis of my lecture is that the Constitution has been essentially ir-relevant to the judgments of the United States Supreme Court in the areas desig-nated freedom of religion and separation of church and state. I would quickly add, moreover, that my allegation regarding the irrelevance of the Constitution is not limited to the interpretation of the so-called religion clauses of the first amendment. The cases decided under that rubric are but examples, and not the most egregious examples at that, of the Court's substitution of its judgment for those of the founding fathers. Perhaps my tale is no more than still another version of *The Emperor's New Clothes,* but I have never been sure of the proper moral to be derived from that story. Was it that the child pierced the propaganda that had brainwashed the populace? Or was it that the adult population demonstrated more civility than could be expected from a child by indulging the Emperor in his peculiar form of exhibitionism?

• • • • • •

Three distinct historical bases on which to ground the meaning of the religion clauses have been articulated. The so-called Madisonian position was that govern-ment should abstain from interference with religious belief or behavior so that each religious faction could compete on its own for adherents. For Madison, the multiplication of religious factions would assure freedom of each and the domi-nance of none. To Thomas Jefferson is attributed the "wall of separation theory," utilized in the several opinions in the *Everson* case, which sees the establishment clause as requiring strict separation of church and state for the protection of the state. The third theory, labeled with Roger Williams' name, calls for the separation of church and state, but only to protect the church against corruption by the state.

So far as the Supreme Court has chosen to assert which of these three con-structions best bottoms the provisions of the religion clauses, it is clear that the Court first opted for the Jeffersonian "wall of separation," with such holes in the wall as it may desire to imagine or create. As Shakespeare put it: "Thou wall, O wall! O sweet and lovely wall! Show me thy chink to blink through with mine eyne." In 1970, however, the Court seemed to have veered to the Williams' argu-ment in *Walz v. Tax Commission* and has wobbled ever since.

The choice of the Jeffersonian wall with its notion of an absolute ban on any government practice that "aids or opposes" any religion, rather than the Williams wall with a one-way door that would allow aid to religion but not infringement on religion, roused the ire of modern churchmen, most notably that of the late Professor Mark DeWolfe Howe and Professor Wilber G. Katz. I quote at length from Katz quoting Howe, lest any paraphrase that I may offer should be affected by my personal bias toward the Jeffersonian approach:

Professor Howe's views were expressed in a series of lectures published under the title *The Garden and the Wilderness*. His criticism could scarcely have been more severe. He charged that "By superficial and purposive interpretations of the past, the Court has dishonored the arts of the historian and degraded the talents of the lawyer." His principal complaint was that the Court's Establishment Clause doctrine was spun exclusively out of the Jeffersonian threads in American church-state tradition. The Court erroneously assumed that the framers of the First Amendment "spoke in a wholly Jeffersonian dialect." Howe's thesis was that the American tradition of church-state separation includes not only the Jeffersonian threads, but also those running back to Roger Williams. Both Jefferson and Williams wrote metaphorically of a wall of separation, but they viewed the wall as serving quite different ends. Howe described the Jeffersonian principle of separation as rooted in deistic rationalism and anticlericalism, Church and state should be separated "as the safeguard of public and private interests against ecclesiastical depradations and excursions." Following this view, the Court seemed to have assumed that "the First Amendment intended to keep alive the bias of the Enlightenment which asserted that government must not give its aid in any form to religion lest impious clerks tighten their grip upon the purses and the minds of men."

. . . Williams' wall protected churches not only against restraints but also against the corrupting effects of the government support. Williams and his followers believed that "the spiritual freedom of churches is jeopardized when they forget the principle of separation."

In Howe's judgment, the First Amedment's prohibitions: . . . at the time of their promulgation were generally understood to be more the expression of Roger Williams' philosophy than of Jefferson's . . . [T] he predominant concern at the time when the First Amendment was adopted was not the Jeffersonian fear that if it were not enacted, the federal government would aid religion and thus advance the interest of impious clerks but rather the evangelical hope that private conscience and autonomous churches, working together and in freedom, would extend the rule of truth.

The Williams principle of separation does not forbid all governmental aids to religion, but only those incompatible with full religious freedom.

With all due respect, Howe and Katz are guilty of the same violations of "the arts of the historian" as they condemn in the Court. But they are half right. Little basis exists for the claim that the Jeffersonian "wall of separation" was the guide to the formulation of the first amendment's religion clauses, except that the theory was written by Madison, the Virginian who clearly espoused the Jeffersonian view, at least for Virginia. Equally, support is absent for the argument that the clauses were framed in accordance with the doctrines of Roger Williams. The primary purpose of the amendment was to keep the national government out of religious matters. Madison, the prime mover of the amendment, thought the amendment unnecessary, except to calm the fears of those who worried that without it the national government would be capable of invading the realm of the states, a realm encompassing laws relating to religion. The states were to be unaffected by the amendment. States like Virginia were free to endorse, as they did, what Professor Howe called the Jeffersonian concern to "safeguard . . . public and private interests against ecclesiastical depredations and excursions." Those like Massachusetts were left free to follow the pietistic views of Williams' "dread of the worldly competitions which might consume the churches if sturdy fences against the wilderness were not maintained." No dominant single theory of church-state relations prevailed, except the notion that it was no business of the national government. As Professor Edmund S. Morgan has written:

> In 1776 most colonies collected taxes for support of the ministry, and one church generally got the bulk of the funds, if not all of them, regardless of its size. In the southern colonies it was the Anglican church, in New England the Congregational. During the Revolution, partly because of the new disposition toward equality, the Anglican church everywhere lost its special position, and most states left the churches of every denomination to support themselves by voluntary donation of their members. But the New England states continued their support, still favoring the Congregationalists, in New Hampshire until 1817, in Connecticut until 1818, and in Massachusetts until 1833.

Today's problems regarding a choice between the views of Jefferson and Williams derive not from the language or purpose of the first amendment, but rather from the attempted application of the first amendment's language to state action, even though the amendment was clearly framed not to be applicable to the states at all. And, as I have suggested, there is no part of the history of the fourteenth amendment that provides any guidance whatsoever for the application of the religion clauses to the states. Thus, the constitutional provisions are not reasons for the decisions in the Court's church and state cases, but only an excuse for them. But Howe and Katz are right in their assertion that the Court uses the grab bag of history to choose arguments that support positions reached for reasons other than those which it marshals. This, however, is not different from the Court's general use of legal precedents, picking among them to support conclusions rather than being guided to conclusions by the precedents. That, of course, is easy when there are conflicting precedents to choose from, as there usually are in this area of constitutional law. Sometimes a precedent is thought to be binding, even though it is conceded to be patently wrong, apparently because it dictates a result desired by the Justice who cannot otherwise justify either that result or the precedent.

Having long since abandoned the search for the original meaning of the religion clauses, the Court has come up with a formula for use in measuring the validity of governmental acts claimed to be in conflict with the first amendment. Alas, like Hamlet's reading matter, it is best described as "words, words, words." And as Pascal told us: "The world is content with words; few think of searching into the nature of things."

Some anguish is avoided for the Court, if not for its critics, by treating the religion clauses as two distinct mandates rather than as a single injunction. The determiniation of which clause is involved is accomplished by stamping a label on the case before considering the issues as one invoking either the free exercise clause or the establishment clause. In most situations, of course, to afford a privilege of freedom claimed for adherents to one religion necessarily results in aiding the religion over others or over the nonreligious. The labeling frequently accomplishes what the modernists would write into the Constitution—a provision that where there is a conflict between the free exercise clause and the establishment clause, the free exercise clause should prevail. That no basis exists for such a proposition either in the language, the history, or the avowed purposes of the first amendment is overcome by the argument that such a construction best comports with our contemporary libertarian ethos.

Even with the ease of judgment that derives from the creation of the dichotomy that the Court now indulges, the Court's rulings have resulted in decisions that are hardly compatible with each other. Such inconsistencies as the Court has wrought hardly suggest a constitutional principle that controls the Court's judgments. Unless, of course, it be that constitutional dictum once privately uttered by a deceased Justice: "So long as the principle is clear, what difference does its application make?"

Thus, in the area labelled freedom of religion, sometimes the question that seems to be asked is whether the government action imposes restraints on the individual because of his religious affiliation or practice or whether the imposition derives from grounds distinct from the religious beliefs or affiliations of the persons regulated? Sometimes the question is whether the regulation in fact inhibits freedom of religious exercise, whatever the nonreligious basis for the promulgated regulation? And here, as elsewhere, the right answer depends on the right question.

The decisions reveal that Mormons may be prosecuted for polygamy although it is—or was—mandated by their religion. And Jehovah's Witnesses may be punished for violation of the child labor law by permitting or requiring children to engage in the street sale of literature, as their faith requires. On the other hand, the Amish—and apparently only the Amish—may be exempted from the compulsory education laws because of their religious beliefs.

Adverse economic effects on seventh-day observers resulting from the state's requirement of abstention from business affairs on Sunday are not invasions of religious freedom. But adverse economic effects on seventh-day observers from unemployment compensation laws requiring availability for employment are invasions of religious freedom. And the payment of benefits to those who have done compulsory military service, which is denied to those who have performed compulsory civilian service because of religious conscientious objections to military service, is not an infringement of religious freedom.

While government is precluded from determining the validity of religious beliefs, the courts may determine whether the beliefs are sufficiently religious to qualify for the benefits of the free exercise clause of the first amendment. Some religious beliefs command exemption from military service, while others do not.

The result of all this is not the application of constitutional principles, but the determination of license to violate the laws with impunity wherever the Court is satisfied that the violations are the consequence of sincere religious beliefs that warrant judicial protection. Thus, the Court's most recent decision is that Jehovah's Witnesses are entitled to be free of New Hampshire's command that license plates display the state motto: 'Live Free or Die." But it should be pointed out that the Court derived this freedom, not from the religion clauses alone, but from the undifferentiated application of the entire first amendment.

The Court's behavior in what it labels freedom of religion cases might be compared with the ancient royal prerogative of dispensation, pursuant to which the Crown could exempt individuals from conforming to the laws of Parliament, particularly for reasons of religious affiliation. That the English Bill of Rights deprived the Crown of such authority is regarded only as testimony to the accepted proposition that courts may be entrusted with arbitrary powers that cannot be left to the discretion of executive or legislative branch action. We are never told why.

When we turn to the establishment cases, the Court purports to have a more clearly defined formula for their resolution. As the Court stated in a recent decision:

> The mode of analysis for Establishment Clause questions is defined by the three part test that has emerged from the Court's decisions. In order to pass muster, a statute must have a secular legislative purpose, must have a principal or primary effect that neither advances nor inhibits religion, and must not foster an excessive government entanglement with religion.

It becomes immediately apparent how the labeling of a case may be determinative of its outcome. There is no doubt, for example, that the exemption granted exclusively to the Amish in *Wisconsin v. Yoder* would fall afoul of the establishment clause standards announced by the Court, unless the decision can be distinguished on the grounds that a state court judicial decree rather than a state legislative exemption was at issue. And once again, the connection between the Court's rule and the constitutional mandate is certainly difficult to ascertain, although the excessive entanglement proposition may be traced to the Roger Williams notion and the secular purpose and effect proposition might be derived from the Jeffersonian argument. It should be noted, however, that the three-prong test requires that the government action satisfy each requirement and not simply one of them.

Nevertheless, the three-prong test has resulted in as much confusion and conflict under the establishment clause as the Court's decisions under the free exercise clause. How, for example, can a law which exempts churches from taxes that others must pay be justified as without the purpose or effect of advancing religious interests and without avoiding entanglement? Yet, that was the Court's conclusion in *Walz v. Tax Commission.* A more tortured opinion would be hard to find.

The bulk of the establishment clause cases have been concerned with aid to private schools. And within this narrow but important area there is again no sign of consistency. Seemingly, the supplying of bus transportaton by the government exclusively to parochial school students is valid. So too, may a government make books available to parochial school students as well as public school students without violating the establishment clause. It may not afford reimbursement for testing in church sponsored schools if the tests are created and administered by parochial school teachers, but it may do so if the tests are state created. So too, may the state provide funds for "diagnostic speech and hearing services and diagnostic psychological services," as well as "physician, nursing, dental, and optometric services in non-public schools." Governmental supply of "therapeutic services" off the school premises does not violate the establishment clause, but the provision of such services on the school premises would. Although "released time" for catechism classes on school premises has been held invalid, "released time" for catechism classes off school premises has been held valid.

If government may supply textbooks to parochial school students, it may not supply other instructional materials—even when they are "incapable of diversion to religious use." Funding for school field trips is invalid, although it provides no more than transportation, because field trips involve an educational function and not, as in *Everson,* merely transportation to school. Providing funds to a religious school, or its students or their parents violates the establishment clause, even if the funds are usable only for maintenance and repairs of buildings. All of this because "[i]n view of the impossibility of separating the secular education function from the sectarian, the state aid inevitably flows in part in support of the religious role of the schools."

It may equally be said of church related colleges and universities that "[i]n view of the impossibility of separating the secular education function from the sectarian, the state aid inevitably flows in part in support of the religious role of the schools." Yet, the Court has made it quite clear that both the national and state governments are free to dispense large sums of money to these colleges and universities so long as the moneys are not directly used for sectarian purposes.

The entanglement part of the Court's triad is either empty or nonsensical. If entanglement means intercourse between government and religious institutions, then no law is more entangling than that which imposes governmental regulation on private schools as all compulsory education laws do. *Pierce v. Society of Sisters* forbade state monopoly of lower school education but implicitly commanded that the state set and enforce proper standards of secular education for parochial schools. The oversight demanded by these laws is certainly far greater than in the public aid to private school statutes that the Court has struck down.

If entanglement means the avoidance of conflict between religious factions over public issues, it says only that state regulation of, or contribution to, religious institutions will be limited to that which the public will placidly tolerate. By this test, the Supreme Court's own opinions in the school prayer cases and in the abortion cases would themselves be violations of the first amendment.

The word entanglement is only an antonym for separation. The former assures no more guidance than the latter. The Court is left to decide how much separation is required or how much entanglement is too much entanglement. Once again, we are reminded of Professor Thomas Reed Powell's comments on the creation of a Restatement of the Commerce Clause: "In the usual form, the black-letter text would read: 'Congress may regulate interstate commerce.' A comment would add: 'The states may also regulate interstate commerce, but not too much.' And then, there would follow a caveat: 'How much is too much is beyond the scope of this Restatement.' " We may also be reminded of Powell's remark when, in introducing Harlan Fiske Stone at a *Columbia Law Review* dinner, he said that Justice Stone was "neither partial, on the one hand, nor impartial, on the other." When we learn to parse that, we may also find the key to the Court's entanglement language.

The primary purpose and primary effect language lead us little way toward any fixed rule. Clearly the primary purpose and the primary effect of the New York tax exemption for church property in *Walz* was to aid the churches or their adherents. That was not only its primary purpose and effect, it was its sole purpose and effect. But it was held to have passed the test.

It is clear that the Court expects that both the purpose and effect requirements be met before a state law can pass muster under the establishment clause. Should a law passed with the purpose of helping religious institutions, but which in fact did not do so, be considered a violation of the first amendment? True, we have seen the Court, for better or worse, pick up the notions of intent—which may be different from purpose—as the essence of a constitutional violation, as in recent racial segregation cases, for example. But it is even less clear why we should be concerned in the church-state cases with unlawful motives rather than unlawful acts. Perhaps, if the road to hell is paved with good intentions, the road to constitutional violations is paved with bad ones.

In any event, the three-prong test hardly elucidates the Court's judgments. Nor does it cover the plastic nature of the judgments in this area. Judicial discretion, rather than constitutional mandate, controls the results.

The lack of principles, no less constitutional principles, in these cases was plainly acknowledged by both Justice Powell and Justice Stevens in the recent case of *Wolman v. Walter.* Justice Stevens would eliminate the chaos by returning to the absolutism of the Jeffersonian wall, but not without acknowledging the Roger Williams argument, because for him the two result in the same end. Although one may wish that Stevens had relied on better authority than the argument of Clarence Darrow in *Scopes v. State,* his position was a demand for consistency:

> The line drawn by the Establishment Clause of the First Amendment must also have a fundamental character. It should not differentiate between direct and indirect subsidies, or between instructional materials like globes and maps on the one hand and instructional materials like textbooks on the other.

He would return to the statement, but not the ruling, of Justice Black in *Everson:* "Under that test, a state subsidy of sectarian schools is invalid regardless of the form it takes." Nevertheless, he, too, would draw lines that would permit public health services and, perhaps, even public diagnostic and therapeutic services, although he had "some misgivings on this [latter] point." But for him, the "Court's efforts to improve on the *Everson* test have not proved successful. 'Corrosive precedents' have left us without firm principles on which to decide these cases." Justice Stevens' resort to Roger Williams' theory may be found in a footnote, where he said:

> In *Roemer v. Maryland Public Works Bd.,* . . . I spoke of 'the pernicious tendency of a state subsidy to tempt religious schools to compromise their religious mission without wholly abandoning it.' This case presents an apt illustration. To qualify for aid, sectarian schools must relinquish their religious exclusivity. As the District Court noted,

the statute provides aid 'to pupils attending only those nonpublic schools whose admission policies make no distinction as to . . . creed . . . of either its pupils or of its teachers . . .' Similarly, sectarian schools will be under pressure to avoid textbooks which present a religious perspective on secular subjects, so as to obtain the free textbooks provided by the State.

Because parochial schools do not have a single function, a religious mission only, the problem of aid to private schools exists. A parochial school is not a church. It is, indeed, required to provide an adequate education in secular subjects as measured by state law. It must be accredited as a grammar school in order for its pupils to attend without violating the compulsory education laws. It is performing a state function as well as a religious function. It is not a place of worship; it is a school. And this is the reason that Justice Powell would abide by the implicit inconsistencies in the rules that his brethren have established as the law of the establishment clause. Justice Powell wrote in *Wolman*:

Our decisions in this troubling area draw lines that often must seem arbitrary. No doubt we could achieve greater analytical tidiness if we were to accept the broadest implications of the observation in *Meek v. Pittenger* . . . that "(s)ubstantial aid to the educational function of (sectarian) schools . . . necessarily results in aid rather than the institutions . . . The persistent desire of a number would become impossible to sustain state aid of any kind—even if the aid is wholly secular in character and is supplied to the pupils rather than the institutions . . . The persistent desire of a number of States to find proper means of helping sectarian education to survive would be doomed. This Court has not yet thought that such a harsh result is required by the Establishment Clause. Certainly few would consider it in the public interest. Parochial schools, quite apart from their sectarian purpose, have provided an educational alternative for millions of young Americans: they often afford wholesome competition with our public schools; and in some States they relieve substantially the tax burden incident to the operation of public schools. The State has, moreover, a legitimate interest in facilitating education of the highest quality for all children within its boundaries, whatever school their parents have chosen for them.

Although accepting the reason behind the first amendment's religion clauses supplied by his fellow Virginians, Jefferson and Madison, Justice Powell further suggests that the wall should nevertheless be torn down, at least a little way:

It is important to keep these issues in perspective. At this point in the 20th century we are quite far removed from the dangers that prompted the Framers to include the Establishment Clause in the Bill of Rights . . . The risk of significant religious or denominational control over our democratic processes—or even of deep political division along religious lines—is remote, and when viewed against the positive contributions of sectarian schools, any such risk seems entirely tolerable in light of the continuing oversight of this Court. Our decisions have sought to establish principles that preserve the cherished safeguard of the Establishment Clause without resort to blind absolutism. If this endeavor means a loss of some analytical tidiness, then that too is entirely tolerable.

These are strange words to be heard from Justice Powell, for they tell us two different things. First, that the religion clauses were meant to prevent evils that no longer threaten. Second, that the principles of the first amendment's religion clauses can be dispensed with so long as whatever violations which may occur are subject "to the continuing oversight of" the Supreme Court. What is in the "public interest" is to be measured, not by constitutional rules, but by judicial "oversight."

It would seem to me, however, that if the Constitution is to be rewritten by the judiciary, it should be written in terms of principles and not by way of ad hoc judgments to which no principle seems applicable. Many years ago, when I was young and naive, I wrote a piece describing what I thought was a principled constitutional ground for application of the religion clauses. Strangely enough, now that I am old and cynical, I still think there is merit in what I said then.

My suggestion was based on the proposition that the religion clauses were not separate mandates but a single one and that the underlying proposition was assurance of equality of treatment. I said then:

> The freedom and separation clauses should be read as stating a single precept: that government cannot utilize religion as a standard for action or inaction because these clauses, read together as they should be, prohibit classification in terms of religion either to confer a benefit or to impose a burden.

That proposition met with almost uniform rejection. The strong adherents to religious faith damned it or ignored it. The freedom riders ridiculed it. Even so tolerant a critic as Professor Giannella would amend it beyond recognition. And certainly the Supreme Court refused to have anything to do with it. Forgive me then if I sin by continuing to take pride in it. But it is not mere pride of authorship or stubbornness that leads me to this adherence—not that I lack either quality. I still think it best represents the meaning of the words and the intention of the authors of the amendment, certainly those of James Madison and Samuel Livermore. It still offers a proper rationalization for most of the cases that the Court has decided. It still offers a basis for the principled application that the Constitution would seem to demand. It would not resolve all questions, for there would necessarily remain, for example, the issue of what is religion? But that question is present whatever construction is given to the religion clauses.

●　●　●　●　●　●

CHAPTER 5   "Criminal Procedure, the Burger Court, and the Legacy of the Warren Court"*

JEROLD H. ISRAEL**

Richard Nixon's criticism of the Warren Court during the 1968 presidential campaign centered largely on the Court's handling of cases involving criminal rights. According to candidate Nixon, the Court had gone much too far. It had twisted the Constitution to serve its own purposes, created a maze of legal technicalities that worked only to frustrate legitimate law enforcement efforts, and so weakened "the peace forces as against the criminal forces in this country" as to be largely responsible for the sharp rise in crime that had occurred in the sixties.

What had to be done, continued Nixon, was to appoint persons to the federal bench "who will interpret the Constitution strictly and fairly and objectively." Such "strict constructionist" judges could be expected not only to put and end to the creation of further legal rights for the accused, but might even trim back on some of the Warren Court "excesses." Decisions such as *Mapp v. Ohio* (1961), prohibiting the use of evidence obtained in violation of the Fourth Amendment's stricture against "unreasonable searches and seizures" and *Miranda v. Arizona* (1966), requiring the police to inform suspects of their constitutional rights before beginning any questioning were frequently cited by Nixon as examples of the type of decisions that should not have been made.

* Copyright ©1977 *Michigan Law Review*. Reprinted by permission. This article is excerpted and printed without footnotes from the *Michigan Law Review*, Volume 75, pp. 1319-1425.
** Professor of Law, Univeristy of Michigan Law School.

Nixon was not the only critic of *Mapp* and *Miranda*. Even certain supporters of the Warren Court had admitted that *Mapp* and *Miranda* were among the Court's "self-inflicted wounds." *Miranda*, for one thing, read more like a piece of legislation than a judicial opinion and *Mapp* recalled only too well Justice Cardozo's famous query: "Is the criminal to go free because the constable has blundered?"

Despite Nixon's victory in 1968 and his appointment of four justices to the Supreme Court, *Mapp* and *Miranda* have not been overruled.

The way in which they have survived and the manner in which the Burger Court has responded to other questions of criminal law and procedure give us another insight into the Burger Court.

The following excerpts are from a lengthy article by University of Michigan Law Professor Jerold H. Israel comparing the Burger and Warren Courts. The selection that follows focuses on his commentary on the Burger Court.

During the 1960s, the Warren Court's decisions in the field of criminal procedure were strongly denounced by many prosecutors, police officers, and conservative politicians. Some of these critics were careful in their description of the Warren Court's record. Others let their strong opposition to several of the Court's more highly publicized decisions destroy their perception of the Court's work as a whole. They characterized the Court's record in terms that can only be described as grossly exaggerated. They accused the Warren Court of ignoring totally the "balanced approach" to criminal procedure that had been taken by its predecessor, the Vinson Court. They claimed that the Warren Court's decisions were concerned only with the protection of the suspect. The Court had ignored, they argued, the fact that encroachment upon liberty could come from two sources; while the government interferes with our liberty when it misuses its law enforcement authority, as the Warren Court's opinions constantly noted, criminals also interfere with our liberty when they commit crimes that deprive us of life, liberty, and property. The Warren Court, the critics asserted, in seeking to deter governmental violations of individual liberty, had failed to give any weight to society's need to combat effectively this criminal element that poses an even greater danger to individual liberty. As a result, the critics claimed, the Warren Court had continuously imposed new limitations on police and prosecutors that had handcuffed those law enforcement officials in their efforts to control crime.

While there may have been some cause for the basic concerns of these critics, they so overstated their case as to create a grossly inaccurate and unfair image of the Warren Court. Fortunately, various civil libertarians, particularly those in academe, sought to set the record straight. They did not necessarily defend the

Court. Indeed, many expressed concern over the quality of the Court's opinions. But they stressed that the critics had greatly exaggerated the extent of the Warren Court's departure from past precedent. The Court had not consistently ignored precedent; indeed, many of its decisions simply built upon past decisions. Neither had the Warren Court decisions looked solely to safeguarding the rights of the accused. The critics had ignored various decisions in which the Warren Court had accepted as constitutional the expansion of police authority to permit more effective law enforcement. Moreover, many of the "liberal" decisions cited by the critics were the product of a doctrinal shift that was related to individual rights generally and not just to the interests of the accused.

Today the tide has turned. The Court of the 1970's—the Burger Court—also is being denounced by various commentators, but now the challenge comes from the civil libertarians. Again some of the critics present a fair portrayal of the Court's record. But others are showing that gross exaggeration is a quality that can be shared by criticisms coming from both sides of the political spectrum. As with the Warren Court critics, many of the Burger Court critics are claiming that the Court has discarded precedent and tradition and has looked to only one aspect of the criminal justice process. They portray the Burger Court as steadily rejecting or "whittling down" the great civil libertarian advances of the Warren Court. They contend that the Burger Court is substituting narrow, technical interpretations of constitutional guarantees for the expansive interpretations of those guarantees adopted by the Warren Court. The current Supreme Court, they argue, shows only a "law and order" orientation—an interest in promoting the enforcement of the law without regard to protecting the rights of the accused. As they see it, the Burger Court has brought the criminal law revoluation of the 1960s to a halt and has, indeed, started a counterrevolution.

Criticism of this type appears to me to be as overstated as was much of the criticism of the Warren Court. The record indicates that the Burger Court has not undermined most of the basic accomplishments of the Warren Court in protecting civil liberties; neither has the Burger Court consistently ignored the interests of the accused. The current critics fail, I believe, to put in proper perspective what the Warren Court did and what the Burger Court has done (or even threatens to do). Certainly, to one who was a strong supporter of the Warren Court decisions in the criminal procedure field, the Burger Court may be somewhat disappointing. But it strikes me that the civil libertarians who describe the current Court as a disaster and a threat to the liberties of individuals are allowing their disappointment to blur their vision.

• • • • • •

Equality and the Burger Court

Has the Burger Court departed substantially from the Warren Court's emphasis upon equality? In two instances the Burger Court has refused to extend the *Griffin* concept. The first, *Ross v. Moffit,* rejected a proposed expansion of the right to appointed counsel on appeal. As noted earlier, the Warren Court held in *Douglas v. California* that the equal protection clause guaranteed the indigent defendant appointed counsel on appeal, but *Douglas* was limited specifically to an initial appeal automatically granted to the defendant under state law. In *Ross* the Burger Court held that *Douglas* would not be expanded to require appointed counsel to assist the indigent in preparing an application for a second-or third-level appellate review that could be granted only at the discretion of the appellate court.

While the Warren Court might have been willing to extend *Douglas* to the *Ross* setting, the *Ross* ruling hardly placed a major limitation on the extension of the *Griffin-Douglas* doctrine. The Court's opinion emphasized that the decision of an appellate court to grant discretionary review rests largely on factors readily apparent from the record below, and therefore counsel's services are not nearly as significant in preparing the application for discretionary review as in presenting the initial appeal, which was treated in *Douglas*. This emphasis could readily be used to distinguish various other aspects of counsel's services that are much more commonly recognized as needed for meaningful access to the judicial process than "the somewhat arcane art of preparing petitions for discretionary review." Indeed, if a state supreme court or the United States Supreme Court exercised its discretion to grant a second- or third-level review, the equal protection clause still would appear to require that the indigent defendant be provided the assistance of counsel in presenting that appeal, since there is much greater need for counsel to present the merits on an appeal than to perform the narrower function involved in *Ross*.

In *United States v. MacCollom*, the Burger Court also refused to expand the *Griffin* analysis, but again the Court's ruling was quite limited. *MacCollom* held that it was constitutionally permissible to require as a condition for providing a free trial transcript on a collateral attack of a conviction, that the trial judge certify that the defendant's claim is not frivolous. The Court stressed, however, that the defendant could have obtained a transcript automatically on direct appeal, without trial court certification. It therefore seems unlikely that *MacCollom* will have significance aside from the special situation presented there, in which the defendant fails to appeal but subsequently seeks to obtain review by collateral attack.

In contrast to *Ross* and *MacCollom*, the Burger Court has approved substantial extensions of the equality theme in other contexts. Most significantly, in *Argersinger v. Hamlin*, the Court extended the *Gideon* ruling to require appointed trial counsel in all misdemeanor cases in which jail sentence is imposed. Moreover, the opinion of the Court left open the possibility of further expanding the right to counsel to encompass some cases in which jail sentences are not imposed. The practical impact of the *Argersinger* decision has been greater than *Gideon*.

Not only are many more cases presented at the misdemeanor level, but there also were many more states that had not been appointing counsel in misdemeanor cases involving jail sentences prior to *Argersinger* than there were states that had not been appointing counsel in felony cases before *Gideon.*

The Burger Court also has approved other extensions of *Gideon.* In *Coleman v. Alabama,* the Court held that, although the state was not required to provide a preliminary hearing, it had to provide appointed counsel when such a hearing was available under state law—even in a jurisdiction that prosecuted by indictment so that the preliminary hearing bindover was not essential. In *Gagnon v. Scarpelli,* the Burger Court held that the indigent person also had a right to the assistance of appointed counsel in various probation and parole revocation proceedings. In *Procunier v. Martinez,* the Court held that a prisoner could not be kept from utilizing the legal assistance of law students and paraprofessionals.

Of course, these decisions do not move entirely in one direction. Liberals may complain that the Burger Court has not gone as far as the Warren Court would have gone on these issues. Maybe so, but maybe not. For example, in *Gagnon,* the Court admittedly did not hold that the indigent had an automatic right to counsel in all parole and probation revocation proceedings; rather, it held that the circumstances of the case would control under an analysis similar to the *Betts v. Brady* analysis that the Warren Court rejected in *Gideon* when it established an automatic right to appointed counsel at trial. Yet it should be noted that Justices Brennan and Marshall, who were both stalwarts of the liberal majority of the Warren Court, accepted the *Gagnon* standard.

In sum, considering *Ross* and *MacCollom* on the one hand, and *Argersinger,* *Gagnon,* and related cases on the other, the civil libertarian critics appear to be on less than firm ground if their broadside condemnation of the Burger Court's treatment of Warren Court precedent is meant to suggest that the Burger Court has undermined, or even generally refused to extend, the equality theme of the Warren Court.

• • • • • •

The Burger Court Record

Expansionism and the Burger Court

There are at least two areas where the Burger Court has taken the lead from the Warren Court and adopted constitutional standards that are as protective of the individual as any the Warren Court would likely have adopted. The Court's interpretation of the sixth amendment right to counsel is one such area. I have already noted the Burger Court decisions in *Argersinger* and *Coleman.* In addition, there is *Faretta v. California,* where the Court held that the right to counsel included a supplemental right of the defendant to proceed pro se at trial, even if he has no special legal knowledge or skill.

Morrissey v. Brewer is another illustration of a ruling at least equally as expansive as many of the Warren Court rulings so warmly praised by civil libertarians. Indeed, Chief Justice Berger's opinion in *Morrissey,* in its extension of basic guarantees beyond the criminal trial, is reminiscent of the Warren Court's ruling in *In re Gault. Morrissey* required, as an element of due process, that significant hearing rights be afforded convicted persons in parole and probation revocation proceedings. Those hearing rights included not only a final hearing (in which the individual is entitled to written notice, disclosure of the evidence against him, a general right of confrontation, and a written statement by the factfinder), but also a preliminary hearing, which has to be provided promptly and must include a limited right to confrontation and notice.

Admittedly, in most areas the Burger Court's record does not show as consistent an emphasis on expansive interpretations as is found in *Morrissey* or in the right-to-counsel cases. Instead, the pattern of the Burger Court decisions tends to be more like that of the Warren Court in dealing with search and seizure problems; expansive interpretations of a particular constitutional guarantee have been adopted in some cases and rejected in others. Nevertheless, a close analysis of its decisions suggests that the Burger Court, on balance, has tended to favor somewhat expansive interpretations of constitutional guarantees in areas other than those involving police investigatory practices. The Court's decisions dealing with the right to a jury trial, double jeopardy, the right to a speedy trial, and the procedural forfeiture of constitutional objections are . . . illustrative of the Court's record in areas marked by this mixed pattern of decisions.

• • • • • •

The Burger Court and Police Practices

So far I have put to one side the Burger Court decisions regulating police investigatory practices. Undoubtedly these decisions have caused the most concern among civil libertarian critics of the Court. That concern is not unexpected. The Warren Court decisions relating to police practices rank high among those Warren Court decisions most revered by civil libertarians. Moreover, it is in this area that the Burger Court most clearly has departed from Warren Court precedents. The question remains, however, whether these Burger Court decisions have, as the critics suggest, largely eviscerated the Warren Court rulings. I believe that this has not been the case to date, and even those further cutbacks that are most likely to be made in the future should not have that effect.

• • • • • •

Police Interrogation

The *Miranda* decision is the most highly publicized of all the Warren Court's criminal procedure decisions, and it is quite understandable that the civil libertarians look to its continuing vitality as a bellwether. In *Miranda,* the Warren Court required exclusion of a defendant's statement obtained through custodial interrogation unless he had been informed of his constitutional rights and of the possible adverse use of the statement (the so-called *"Miranda* warnings") and had voluntarily waived those rights before making the statement. Although the value of the *Miranda* ruling in effectively protecting the suspect's self-incrimination privilege is debatable, the decision has a symbolic quality that extends far beyond its practical impact upon police interrogation methods.

As noted previously, a major element of the *Miranda* decision—the equal treatment of the indigent—has not suffered at the hands of the Burger Court. Other aspects of the decision have, perhaps, been treated less well. Yet, the fact remains that *Miranda* still is the law of the land. Moreover, while its ramifications arguably have been narrowed, the Court has not cast doubt upon its basic premise that the defendant's right against self-incrimination applies to police custodial interrogation and not just to judicial compulsion of testimony by the threat of contempt. The Burger Court decisions most frequently noted by critics as undermining the *Miranda* ruling—*Harris v. New York, Michigan v. Tucker, Michigan v. Mosley,* and *Oregon v. Mathiason*—all have accepted that basic assumption.

Harris permitted the use of statements obtained in violation of *Miranda* to impeach the defendant's trial testimony. In the *Tucker* case, although the Court dealt with a special situation relating to retroactive application of *Miranda*, it clearly raised the possibility that the testimony of "tainted witnesses"—*i.e.,* witnesses who were discovered because of a statement obtained in violation of *Miranda* —would not be excluded from evidence. In the *Mosley* decision, the Court held that a second interrogation session that occurred after a suspect initially refused to make a statement did not violate *Miranda* under the facts of that case. In the recent *Mathiason* case, the Court noted that not all interrogation conducted in a police station is necessarily "custodial interrogation" (the only type of questioning subject to *Miranda*).

While none of these cases adopted the expansive view of *Miranda* that the civil libertarians would have preferred, it also is true that *Tucker, Mathiason,* and perhaps even *Mosley* did not significantly detract from the basic *Miranda* ruling. The Court's conclusion in *Mathiason* that the suspect there had not been in "custody" might well have been reached by the members of the *Miranda* majority themselves. The suspect voluntarily came to the police station after a police officer requested that they meet; he was immediately informed that he was not under arrest; and he was allowed to leave following the close of the interview, even though he admitted committing the crime. While Justice Marshall dissented, his major point was that the Court should go beyond the custodial interrogation situation covered in *Miranda* and reach other interrogation situations as well.

Tucker, on the facts presented, also can be squared with *Miranda*. The issue before the Court concerned the application of the fruit-of-the-poisonous-tree doctrine to the testimony of a witness discovered as a result of police interrogation that had violated the *Miranda* requirements, but had been conducted before the *Miranda* case was decided. The Court held that, in light of the special problems raised by the application of *Miranda* to pre-*Miranda* interrogations, it was inappropriate to expand the impact of retroactive application by excluding the witness' testimony as well as the defendant's statement. However, language in Justice Rehnquist's majority opinion suggests that the Burger Court might not extend the poisoned-fruits doctrine to the tainted witness even where retroactive application is not involved. Assuming the Court eventually takes that position, would it necessarily be inconsistent with *Miranda*, especially where the police interrogation was not designed specifically to obtain the names of witnesses? Some very "liberal" judges have acknowledged that the extension of the poisoned-fruits doctrine to subsequently discovered witnesses who willingly cooperate with the police is at least a very difficult question. While the witness may have been found through the defendant's statement, the possibility always exists that he might otherwise have come to the attention of the police if they had reached the point of methodically tracking down all persons who had even the remotest link to the victim of the accused. Indeed, even where the witness could not have been found by the most intensive investigation, the possibility remains that the witness eventually might have come forward on his own, perhaps in response to a general police request for assistance.

Mosley is similar to *Tucker* in that the decision was based on a rather unusual situation. The Court in *Mosley* upheld a second interrogation session after the defendant initially had refused to waive his rights and speak with officers. In rejecting the defendant's claim that *Miranda* prohibited a second attempt to obtain his waiver, the Court stressed the particular facts surrounding the second interrogation in *Mosley*. The second interrogation related to a separate crime and was initiated by an officer who apparently had not been aware of the defendant's initial refusal to cooperate. The officer had given complete *Miranda* warnings at the outset of the second session, and the defendant in no way indicated that he did not want to discuss the second crime. Admittedly, Justice White, in a concurring opinion, advanced an interpretation of *Miranda* that generally would allow repeated attempts to interrogate following an initial refusal, but his opinion was not joined by any of the other justices.

Unlike *Mosley, Tucker,* or *Mathiason, Harris v. New York,* the impeachment case, clearly did impose a significant limit upon the impact of *Miranda*. From the prosecutor's viewpoint, the consequences of a *Miranda* violation may be softened considerably by the ability to use the defendant's statement for impeachment purposes. A major value in obtaining a statement from a defendant, even where the defendant does not acknowledge commission of the offense, is the discovery provided regarding the defendant's likely trial testimony. While the defendant may shift somewhat from the explanation in his statement, the statement's availability for impeachment should keep the defendant's testimony close to that original explanation. Of course, if the statement is incriminating, then the *Harris* ruling is likely to have even more value from the prosecution's viewpoint. It may place the defendant in a position where he will be forced to take the chance involved in not testifying at all. If he takes the stand, the statement surely will be damaging notwithstanding the judge's admonition to the jury that they can consider the incriminating admissions only as to impeachment and not as substantive evidence.

Harris thus may be quite significant from the prosecutor's point of view. It is the police, however, who are largely responsible for determining how *Miranda* will be applied, and their immediate objectives focus more on justifying a decision to go forward with the prosecution than on the trial techniques eventually used to win the case. An admissible incriminating statement is of immense value in building the prima facie case needed to gain approval of the prosecution. A statement obtained in violation of *Miranda*, on the other hand, is likely to be given very little weight in determining whether a prosecution should be carried forward. The primary emphasis at this point must be on the adequacy of the prima facie case needed to get the case to the jury, not on certain tactical advantages that may be available if the defendant is forced to present a defense. Thus, from the police viewpoint, *Harris* does not substantially alter the impact of a *Miranda* violation.

It thus seems likely that, insofar as police compliance with *Miranda* is determined by the officer's calculated evaluation of the costs of violation, *Harris* should not influence significantly the officer's decision. Of course, *Harris* could have a substantial impact if it led prosecutors and others involved in police training programs to place less emphasis on compliance with *Miranda*, since police adherence to *Miranda* probably is influenced far more by the general thrust of that training than by calculated cost-benefit evaluations made by officers in individual cases. I am not aware, however, of any such change in training programs, and the continuing symbolic and practical significance of *Miranda* makes it most unlikely that *Harris* alone would encourage such a change.

• • • • • •

Search and Seizure

Civil libertarians also have expressed considerable concern over the Burger Court's treatment of the fourth amendment. Indeed, the Court's decisions relating to the constitutionality of searches and seizures probably have been more sharply criticized than any other group of decisions involving the regulation of police practices. That criticism has centered primarily upon two sets of decisions, one defining the substantive standards for determining the reasonableness of a search or arrest and the other defining the scope of the exclusionary rule adopted in *Mapp v. Ohio.*

The resonableness of a search or arrest. In evaluating the Burger Court decisions dealing with the substantive standards for searches and seizures, it should be recalled that the Warren Court decisions in this area were varied in approach. On the one hand, the Warren Court refused to adopt expansive interpretations of the fourth amendment in several major decisions. In *Warden v. Hayden*, for example, the Court rejected the long-standing interpretation of the fourth amendment as prohibiting searches for "mere evidence." In *Terry v. Ohio*, the Court rejected the contention that frisks must be justified by probable cause. *Ker v. California* recognized that no-knock entry was permissible where needed to prevent the likely destruction of evidence. In *McCray v. Illinois*, the Court rejected a defense contention that, in challenging the probable cause allegedly supporting the search, it had the right to discover the name of the anonymous tipster who furnished information that led to the search. On the other hand, there were various decisions in which the Warren Court did adopt new, more rigorous standards for acceptable searches. Several cases rejected earlier opinions that had deemphasized the need for warrant authorization of a search whenever practicable. Most notably, *Chimel v. California* limited the permissible scope of a warrantless search incident to an arrest and thereby narrowed one of the most significant exceptions to the warrant requirement. At the same time, *Spinelli v. United States* applied stringent standards to the affidavit submitted on an application for a search warrant, thereby ensuring that the magistrate had an adequate factual foundation for determining whether to grant a warrant.

The Burger Court has on several occasions likewise adopted expansive interpretations of the fourth amendment. Thus, *United States v. United States District Court* held unconstitutional warrantless electronic surveillance of a domestic group accused of violence against the government. The Court held that the substantial governmental interest in a domestic security investigation could not override the traditional fourth amendment standards requiring warrant authorization of electronic surveillance. In *Gerstein v. Pugh,* the Court required alteration of the pretrial practice in many states by holding that the fourth amendment required a prompt post-arrest review of probable cause by a magistrate where an arrest was made without a warrant and the arrestee was still in custody or subject to extended restraint. *Coolidge v. New Hampshire* held invalid a rather unusual state practice that permitted a state attorney general to serve as a magistrate for the purpose of issuing a search warrant.

Decisions such as *District Court, Gerstein,* and *Coolidge* do not reflect the general trend, however. Viewed as a whole, Burger Court decisions judging the reasonableness of searches and seizures generally have refused to adopt new, more rigorous fourth amendment standards. Indeed, as critics have noted, the Burger

Court decisions tend to grant the police more leeway than did the Warren Court decisions. The difference in the positions of the two Courts is not nearly as substantial, however, as the sharp criticism of the current Court might suggest.

In several major areas of search and seizure, it is far from certain that the often-criticized Burger Court decisions reach a conclusion contrary to that which the Warren Court might have reached. Thus, the Burger Court's decision upholding the issuance of a search warrant in *United States v. Harris* arguably may depart from the Warren Court ruling in *Spinelli v. United States,* but it should be noted that Justice White, who was one of the five Justices in the majority in *Spinelli,* also joined *Harris.* The divergence between the two rulings certainly is not extensive, and *Harris* arguably may be viewed as more consistent with the earlier Warren Court decision in *Draper v. United States.*

Similarly, while the Burger Court decisions dealing with probable-cause searches of automobiles arguably have failed to carry forward the *Chimel* emphasis upon obtaining warrant authorization whenever practicable, it seems likely that the Warren Court also would have viewed the *Chimel* rationale as inapplicable to most automobile searches. The leading Burger Court decision limiting the applicability of that rationale for automobile searches, *Chambers v. Maroney,* almost certainly would have been accepted by the Warren Court. Justice Stewart, who wrote *Chimel,* and Justices Douglas, Brennan, and Marshall, who had joined the *Chimel* opinion, all joined the Court's opinion in *Chambers.* They apparently had no difficulty with *Chambers'* extension of the "moving vehicle" exception to the warrent requirement (an exception that *Chimel* had not challenged) to uphold the warrantless search of an automobile conducted after the driver had been arrested and the automobile had been removed to the police station. Only Justice Harlan contended that such an extension was improper since temporary immobilization of the car would afford police ample opportunity to obtain a warrant before beginning their search.

Of course, *Chambers*, in turn, served as the foundation for *Cardwell v. Lewis* and *Texas v. White,* two cases that arguably further expanded the scope of the moving vehicle exception. *Cardwell,* in particular, may have undercut the Court's analysis in *Coolidge v. New Hampshire,* which suggested that the *Chambers* exception was limited to cases involving an unanticipated stopping of an automobile. but *Coolidge,* it must be remembered, was not a Warren Court decision but rather was a 1971 decision in which Justice Stewart's plurality opinion was supported by only three other Justices. Admittedly, Justice Stewart's opinion in *Coolidge* might have received majority support from the Warren Court of the 1962-1969 period, but, even under that assumption, *Cardwell* is the only one of the automobile search cases that clearly would have been decided differently by the Warren Court. Certainly, the *Cardwell* decision standing alone cannot be viewed as a dramatic departure from the Warren Court's position in *Chimel,* once *Chambers* is accepted as a valid exception to that position.

The Burger Court's decision in *Adams v. Williams* presents similar difficulties in assessing its relationship to Warren Court precedent. *Adams* extended the *Terry v. Ohio* ruling on frisks to uphold forcible stops based on reasonable suspicion. Moreover, it did so where the individual's suspicious activity related solely to possessory offenses (narcotics and weapon possession), rather than to a forthcoming crime of violence as was suspected in *Terry*. *Adams* also held that the reasonable suspicion needed for a stop and frisk had been established when a person known to the officer approached the policeman on the street and reported the possessory offense but did not provide further corroboration. Notwithstanding the vigorous dissents of Justice Douglas (who had also dissented in *Terry*) and Justices Brennan and Marshall (who had joined *Terry*), it is certainly arguable that a Warren Court majority would have agreed with *Adams*. Justices Stewart and White, who joined Chief Justice Warren's opinion in *Terry*, also joined in the *Adams* decision, and the *Adams* case fits sufficiently within the basic rationale advanced in *Terry* to suggest that the remainder of the *Terry* majority might have reached a similar result. Although the *Terry* opinion did not rule on forcible stops, it posed an operating procedure that certainly suggested their validity. Similarly, the *Terry* rationale is in no way inconsistent with basing reasonable suspicion on information supplied by third persons without substantial corroboration by the officer's own observations.

More clear-cut deviations from the philosophy of the Warren Court arguably are found in several recent cases that permitted searches without requiring probable cause. In *South Dakota v. Opperman,* the Court upheld warrantless inventory searches of impounded automobiles. *Opperman* was based on a Warren Court precedent, *Cooper v. California*, but it is most unlikely that the Warren Court would have so extended *Cooper*. In *United States v. Robinson* and *Gustafson v. Florida*, the Burger Court upheld full searches of the person incident to a traffic arrest. Arguably, the Warren Court would have agreed with Justice Marshall's dissent in *Robinson*, which contended that no more than a frisk for weapons should be permitted since the officer clearly cannot expect to find evidence of the traffic offense on the person of the arrestee. Here again, however, the majority's position had substantial foundation in earlier opinions. Indeed, the majority opinions in *Robinson* and *Gustafson* may reflect a lesson suggested in several Warren Court opinions—the need for flat, simple rules that can easily be applied by police officers. Arguably, the Warren Court would have found such an approach inappropriate where used to extend police authority, but it should be noted that Justice Stewart, who wrote *Katz* and *Chimel*, two of the leading "liberal" search-and-seizure opinions of the Warren Court, also joined the *Robinson* majority and concurred in the result in *Gustafson*.

Justice Stewart also wrote for the majority in *Schneckloth v. Bustamonte,* another case that arguably deviates from the policy of the Warren Court through its generous interpretation of a doctrine (search by consent) that validates searches without probable cause. *Schneckloth* ruled that, in establishing voluntary consent to a search following a street stop, the prosecution need not show that the individual had been made aware of his right to refuse to consent. The Warren Court presumably would have imposed a heavier burden on the prosecution, as urged in the dissenting opinions of Justices Marshall and Brennan.

Assuming that the decisions in *Opperman, Robinson, Gustafson,* and *Schneckloth* do depart from the approach of the Warren Court, how significant are these decisions in altering the protection of privacy afforded by the fourth amendment? Although all four permit searches without probable cause, they might not substantially broaden the search authority of the police beyond that which the Warren Court would have accepted. In *Robinson* and *Gustafson*, for example, it must be remembered that the dissenters would have permitted an automatic frisk of the arrested person, although not a full search. Moreover, as the dissenters also acknowledged, if the arrestee did not obtain his prompt release on station-house bail, he would have been subjected to an inventory search of his person (although the dissenters would not have permitted an inventory search so thorough as to examine the contents of the cigarette package that contained the contraband seized in *Robinson*). Finally, it also should be noted that *Robinson* and *Gustafson* apply only where the traffic stop involves a full-custody arrest, and Justice Stewart's concurring opinion in *Gustafson* leaves open the possibility that the fourth amendment might not permit full-custody arrests for all traffic violations.

The potential impact of *Opperman* is similarly limited by issues left open in the majority opinion. The inventory search involved there extended only to the interior of the automobile and an unlocked glove compartment. It is uncertain whether the same standard would be applied to a locked glove compartment or trunk. Although the car in *Opperman* was itself locked, it generally is much easier for someone to break into a locked car than into a locked trunk or glove compartment, and the police might have greater justification for removing all valuables from those areas that are readily accessible once the door locks are bypassed.

Like *Robinson* and *Gustafson*, the *Schneckloth* ruling on consent searches also was based upon a "street situation"—the noncustodial, on-the-street stop of an automobile. The *Schneckloth* majority held that, in such a situation, the prosecution does not have to establish that a driver, in granting his consent, was aware that he had a right to refuse the officer's request to search the car. In particular, the majority ruled that the police need not give warnings similar to those required by *Miranda* before requesting consent. It should be noted that the majority opinion does not relieve the prosecution of the burden of showing that the consent was voluntary. Neither does it render the driver's knowledge an irrelevant factor in determining voluntariness. The dissents by Justices Brennan and Marshall rejected the contention that the driver's awareness of the right to refuse to permit the search could be assumed, but, at the same time, neither dissent would have required that the police necessarily inform the driver of his right to refuse to give consent. The practical significance of the distinction between this position and that of the majority is difficult to determine. It is not clear, for example, whether the dissenters would permit the prosecution to establish knowledge by showing simply that the officer's phrasing of the request in itself suggested a right to refuse (*e.g.*, where the officer said, "Will you give me your permission to search?").

No doubt, when decisions like *Opperman, Robinson,* and *Scheckloth* are added to decisions like *Cardwell*, the overall thrust of the Burger Court decisions is to grant the police far more flexibility than a civil libertarian is likely to view as acceptable. Yet the Court's approach is not so substantially different from that taken in many Warren Court decisions as to be characterized as a major departure from the Warren Court's standard. Admittedly, there is a more substantial departure when the comparison is limited to the position taken by Chief Justice Warren and Justices Douglas, Brennan, Marshall, Fortas, and Goldberg. But, for much of the Warren period, no more than four of these Justices sat together, and they could not count on the ready support of Justice Black who often opposed an expansionist view of the fourth amendment. As a result, the Warren Court decisions in this area reflected a varied approach that was perhaps more "conservative" than its approach in other areas. The Burger Court's fourth amendment decisions accordingly come closer in approach to the Warren Court rulings than do the decisions involving other police practices, where the addition of Justice Black gave the Warren Court majority greater leeway.

The scope of the exclusionary rule. As noted above, the civil libertarian critics also have expressed concern as to the Burger Court's treatment of a second aspect of the fourth amendment, the application of the *Mapp v. Ohio* exclusionary rule. So far, the Burger Court has done very little to restrict the *Mapp* ruling itself, which required the exclusion of unconstitutionally seized evidence only at the criminal trial. Indeed, in *Brown v. Illinois*, the Court specifically rejected an invitation to limit sharply the fruit-of-the-poisonous-tree doctrine, which determines the reach of the exclusionary rule in the trial setting. In *Brown*, the Court rejected the contention that the giving of the *Miranda* warnings automatically purged the taint of an illegal arrest, thereby permitting the admissibility of any subsequent confession of the arrestee to be judged without regard to the illegal arrest. The Court also made clear that *Wong Sun v. United States*, a Warren Court decision first holding an incriminating statement inadmissible as the fruit of an illegal arrest, was not limited to the facts of the case, which involved a statement made almost contemporaneously with the arrest.

On the other side, the Burger Court has rejected attempts to extend the exclusionary rule outside of the criminal trial, and it has overturned Warren Court precedent permitting a habeas corpus challenge to a conviction resulting from a trial in which illegally seized evidence was admitted. In *United States v. Calandra*, the Court held that the *Mapp* rule did not extend to grand jury proceedings, and a witness therefore could not object to grand jury questioning based on information obtained through a fourth amendment violation. While Justices Marshall, Brennan, and Douglas dissented, it is not clear that the majority's position would have been rejected by the Warren Court. That Court had accepted in other contexts Justice Black's view that the Court should be most reluctant to impose new legal limitations on grand jury proceedings since such limitations tend to cause delay and impede the grand jury's performance as a safeguard against unjust prosecutions.

In *United States v. Janis*, the Burger Court held that the exclusionary rule did not apply to an IRS assessment proceeding (a civil action) where the illegal search had been conducted by local police. Here, as Justice Stewart's dissent indicates, it is very likely that the Warren Court would have reached a different result. A major function of the exclusionary rule is to deter unconstitutional searches by denying police the use of illegally seized evidence, and the *Janis* ruling arguably might offer a counter-incentive to engage in such searches. However, *Janis* certainly should produce no more than a slight dent in the deterrent impact of the rule, since the primary concern of police remains the obtaining of criminal convictions, not possible IRS assessments.

A similar conclusion might be advanced with regard to *Stone v. Powell.* Here the Court clearly narrowed the exclusionary rule's scope but still left substantially intact its general effectiveness as a deterrent device. *Stone* held that, for all practical purposes, a fourth amendment objection could not be utilized to challenge collaterally a state conviction in a federal habeas corpus proceeding. The majority ruled that a federal court could not consider a habeas claim that unconstitutionally seized evidence was used at the petitioner's trial unless the petitioner had not been afforded an opportunity for "full and fair litigation" of his claim in the state courts. *Stone* rejected several Warren Court decisions that had considered fourth amendment claims on habeas petitions. Moreover, the *Stone* ruling arguably was inconsistent with the reasoning, though not the holding, of *Fay v. Noia*, one of the most celebrated opinions of the Warren era. Although *Fay* dealt with a collateral challenge to a conviction based on a coereced confession, the *Fay* opinion certainly suggested that federal habeas corpus should be available to challenge collaterally a state conviction on any constitutional error.

The Burger Court obviously is concerned about the sharp increase in habeas petitions since *Fay* and is seeking to restrict the scope of that opinion. Like *Stone*, *Francis v. Henderson*, discussed earlier, also narrowed the scope of collateral attack. From a civil libertarian viewpoint, the significance of decisions like *Francis* and *Stone* depends in large part on the importance of federal habeas review in achieving full recognition of the particular constitutional right in question. With respect to *Stone* and the fourth amendment, that significance should relate primarily to the degree to which federal habeas review strengthens the deterrent impact of the exclusionary rule beyond the deterrence that flows from the rule's application in the state courts. While people may disagree as to the precise significance of such federal habeas reinforcement, it surely has a comparatively minor bearing upon the rule's overall effectiveness as a deterrent.

The elimination of a federal collateral challenge based on the fourth amendment hardly is significant enough to suggest to police that the fourth amendment can be ignored. The primary focus of the police is on the everyday application of the exclusionary sanction by state courts. Of course, if the elimination of federal collateral attack led state trial courts to eviscerate fourth amendment standards, that stance probably would lead police, in turn, to pay considerably less attention to the fourth amendment. It seems most unlikely, however, that the *Stone* decision will encourage many state trial courts to vitiate the fourth amendment. The limited number of federal habeas reversals of state convictions suggests that a state trial judge with an inclination to ignore the fourth amendment is likely to be concerned primarily with reversal by a state appellate court, not by a federal habeas court. And the restraining influence of state appellate review should remain substantially intact notwithstanding *Stone*. Admittedly, *Stone* may have some impact upon those state appellate courts that have "liberalized" their views to fit that of the federal circuit court of appeals in their area, but such shifts in position are likely to be far too subtle to have any dramatic impact on trial court (or police) practices.

Taken together, the impact of *Calandra, Janis,* and *Stone* upon *Mapp* appears to be roughly similar to the impact of *Mosley, Tucker,* and *Mathiason* upon *Miranda:* while the Burger Court has refused to extend the *Mapp* ruling, neither has it cut back significantly upon the scope of that ruling. Indeed, as with *Miranda*, the intensity of civil libertarian criticism probably relates less to what the Court has done with the *Mapp* decision than to what the critics fear it will do in the future. Chief Justice Burger has suggested that perhaps *Mapp* simply should be overruled. He appears to stand alone, however, in suggesting total abandonment of the exclusionary rule. A more likely possibility is the modification of *Mapp* suggested by Justice White in *Stone*. There, Justice White urged that unconstitutionally seized evidence need not be excluded where the officer who seized the evidence was "acting in the good-faith belief that his conduct comported with existing laws" and had "reasonable grounds for [that] belief." While it appears that Justice White may have the support of three other Justices for adopting this modification the presence of the additional vote needed for a majority opinion is highly speculative. Let us assume, however, that Justice White's view does prevail. From the viewpoint of the civil libertarian, how much will have been lost? I suggest that the wound will be primarily to the civil libertarian's pride, not to the primary function of the exclusionary rule.

Of course, if one views the exclusion of evidence as an appropriate personal remedy for the person whose privacy has been invaded by an illegal search, then

Justice White's approach has the basic defect of leaving some injured defendants without a remedy. But the Court traditionally has justified the exclusionary rule on two other rationales. Those rationales are the deterrence theory noted above and the theory that exclusion is necessary to maintain "the imperative of judicial integrity"–that courts cannot, consistent with their duty to uphold the Constitution, condone constitutional violations by permitting the fruits of those violations to serve as the basis for criminal convictions. When the exclusionary rule is viewed in light of these theories, Justice White's proposal does not seriously undermine the rule's basic functions, although it certainly does not strengthen the rule.

First, accepting arguendo the judicial-integrity rationale, Justice White's proposed modification would hardly place the Court in a more precarious position in maintaining that integrity than do various current rulings that also allow unconstitutionally seized evidence to be used in judicial proceedings. Consider, for example, the Warren Court ruling in *Alderman v. United States,* which held that a defendant lacks standing to object to the admission of evidence unconstitutionally seized from a third person. Under *Walder v. United States,* an early Warren Court opinion, unconstitutionally seized evidence also could be used under some circumstances for impeachment purposes. If the trial court's failure to exclude illegally seized evidence threatens its integrity by creating the "taint of [judicial] partnership in official lawlessness," it does so as readily under *Alderman* and *Walder* as under Justice White's proposed modification of *Mapp.* Indeed, that proposal, unlike *Alderman,* would at least draw distinctions according to the type of illegality and ensure condemnation of purposeful police illegality.

The impact of Justice White's proposed modification upon the deterrent function of the exclusionary rule is more troublesome. As even the most ardent supporters of the Warren Court acknowledge, the exclusionary rule has obvious limits as an effective deterrent device. The key to the rule's effectiveness as a deterrent lies, I believe, in the impetus it has provided to police training programs that make officers aware of the limits imposed by the fourth amendment and emphasize the need to operate within those limits. Justice White's exclusionary standard is not likely to result in the elimination of such programs, which are now viewed as an important aspect of police professionalism. Neither is it likely to alter the tenor of those programs; the possibility that illegally obtained evidence may be admitted in borderline cases is unlikely to encourage police instructors to pay less attention to fourth amendment limitations. Finally, Justice White's proposal should not encourage officers to pay less attention to what they are taught, as the requirement that the officer act in "good faith" is inconsistent with closing one's mind to the possibility of illegality.

I have considered so far the deterrent impact of the exclusionary rule only insofar as it serves what Professor Andenaes describes as a "general preventive effect." Arguably, the exclusionary rule also may have a significant impact as an immediate threat that deters illegal conduct in a particular case. Although we have come to place less reliance on special deterrence as a justification for imposing criminal sanctions, perhaps the Benthamite model makes sense as applied to the exclusionary rule, since the officer presumably operates in a less emotional, more rational fashion than most criminal offenders. Still, assuming that the rule does have a "special deterrence" effect, Justice White's proposed modification of the rule should not substantially alter that impact in those instances where it is most likely to be significant.

Where the officer recognizes that a search is clearly illegal, the special deterrence effect should not be diluted, since the officer also should recognize that the fruits of the search will be excluded under Justice White's proposal. The proposal is far more likely to have a bearing on those cases in which the officer views the legality of the search as a close question. In such a borderline case, the officer might proceed with the search on the ground that there is a good chance that the evidence will be admitted under Justice White's standard even if the search eventually is found to be illegal. Whether officers are likely to make such careful calculations is questionable. But assuming they do, will the officer's decision to proceed with the search in such borderline cases constitute a substantial change from current behavior? Even under the current *Mapp* rule, are not officers likely to proceed in cases they recognize as borderline, particularly where they are concerned that the evidence may not be available for seizure by the time they cure any potential legal difficulties? If the officer is astute enough to recognize the borderline nature of the search, he also should be astute enough to know that in a truly borderline case the issue of illegality of the search is likely to be compromised in the plea negotiation process, so that some prosecutorial benefit will be obtained from the search in any event.

Justice Brennan has raised still another objection to Justice White's approach: that it could retard the development of search and seizure law. In close cases, Justice Brennan suggests, the state and federal courts will not bother to decide whether the search was illegal, but simply will admit the evidence on the basis of the officer's good-faith effort supported by his reasonable belief as to the validity of the search. It is not clear, however, that Justice White's proposal would permit a court to follow that approach in deciding fourth amendment issues. The trial court readily could be required to determine whether there was, in fact, a violation of the fourth amendment before it begins to examine the officer's good faith. Justice White's approach, like the American Law Institute's similar proposal for modifying *Mapp*, apparently requires consideration of the "extent of [the officer's] deviation from lawful conduct"; the Court could readily hold that, to evalutate that factor, the trial court initially must determine how the requirements of the fourth amendment apply to the case before it.

In sum, the Burger Court has not yet modified *Mapp* as applied to the criminal trial. Moreover, if it should do so, the most likely modification—Justice White's approach—can hardly be described as a threat to the very heart of the rule.

Looking to the area of police practices as a whole, the Burger Court decisions certainly provide a more substantial basis for civil libertarian criticism than the Court's decisions in other areas of criminal procedure. Yet, even in this area, when one considers decisions such as *Gerstein, United States v. United States District Court,* and *Brewer* and notes the limited scope of decisions such as *Mosley* and *Schneckloth,* it seems to be stretching the record to say that the Court has followed a definite pattern of "looking at defendants' rights as narrowly as possible without overruling past decisions." Certainly, statements of utter despair concerning the removal of constitutional restraints upon police can hardly be justified by the Court's decisions to date. Much of that despair undoubtedly relates to antici- pated decisions, but here again, based on reasonable expectations, the critics' concerns appear overstated. While it remains possible that the current majority will overrule *Miranda* and *Mapp,* the Court's recent decisions, and the opinions of the individual Justices, suggest an approach more likely to be directed toward modifications that will not undermine the basic strength of either *Miranda* or *Mapp.*

THE BURGER COURT IMAGE

Where then does this analysis leave us when we review the record of the Burger Court as a whole? Even the most zealous civil libertarian, I suggest, can- not properly characterize the Court's decisions as reflecting an absolute, or even consistent, opposition to an expansionist interpretation of the Bill of Rights' guarantees. Neither can the Court properly be charged with having destroyed, or even having seriously threatened to destroy, the basic legacy of the Warren Court. The selective incorporation doctrine and the concept of equal treatment of the indigent remain firmly implanted in the governing law. Similarly, in deter- mining the scope of individual Bill of Rights' guarantees, the Court has followed the expansionist tendencies of the Warren Court in several areas. Decisions like *Argersinger, Faretta, Morrissey, Ashe, Waller,* and *Taylor* are fully in keeping with the Warren Court tradition. In other areas, the Court's decisions may not have gone as far as the Warren Court would have gone, but they are not far be- hind. The *Barker* decision, for example, may not be as far-reaching as the civil libertarians would have liked, but it has put pressure on the states to make sub- stantial legislative efforts to guarantee a speedy trial to defendants.

Of course, the Burger Court decisions do not move entirely in one direction. There are various cases in which expansionist interpretations have been rejected, and in the area of police practices the Burger Court clearly seems intent upon cutting back upon, though not necessarily overruling, some of the key Warren Court decisions. Yet, taken as a whole, the Burger Court record certainly does not suggest that the Court values effective law enforcement over all else. Indeed, its decisions consistently reject an approach that would permit the state to override the interests of the accused whenever such action could be supported by a rational state interest. A Court that started from Judge Learned Hand's assumptions that "the accused has every advantage" at trial and that the primary defect in the current process is the "archaic formalism and watery sentiment that obstructs, delays, and defeats the prosecution of crime" surely would have rejected the defense claims recognized in such cases as *Wardius, Faretta,* and *Brooks.*

The civil libertarian critics also must take into account the fact that the issues presented to the Burger Court have a somewhat different quality than many of the issues presented to the Warren Court. Although the Warren Court had to treat close questions in several of its most prominent decisions, it also dealt with a significant number of cases that were rather easily resolved once it was decided that the particular constitutional provision applied to the states through the fourteenth amendment. The Burger Court has not had the opportunity to "bolster" its record in the protection of civil liberties with many cases like *Pointer v. Texas, Duncan v. Louisiana, Klopfer v. North Carolina,* and *Benton v. Maryland.* Of course, even if one discounts such decisions, the remaining Warren Court decisions obviously show a more substantial leaning toward an expansive interpretation of individual safeguards than do the Burger Court decisions, particularly in the area of police practices. But the weakness in the Burger Court's record from a civil libertarian's point of view may exist only as compared with the performance of the Warren Court. Even there, the current Court's record is quite comparable to the record of the Warren Court before 1962, when Justice Goldberg replaced Justice Frankfurter. The Burger Court certainly has made far greater advances in protecting the interests of the accused than were made by the Vinson Court, even when appropriate weight is given to the narrow and scarce precedents upon which the Vinson Court could build. Moreover, while civil libertarians have called our attention to several state courts that recently have imposed more rigorous limitations on police or prosecutors pursuant to state constitutions, the fact remains that the Burger Court is ahead of most state courts in protecting civil liberties, as illustrated by the significant change in state practice required by decisions like *Argersinger, Ashe, Waller,* and *Morrissey.*

There remains the contention that the harsh civil libertarian criticism of the Burger Court is justified not so much by what the Court has done, but by what it has said. Even when defense claims are upheld by the Burger Court, it is argued, the opinions raise questions that encourage state court evasion of the Court's own decisions; considerations are balanced so neatly that each case appears limited to its facts; and doubts never before entertained are expressed about the future course of precedent. These qualities undoubtedly are found in several of the Court's leading opinions, but almost all of those are opinions dealing with *Mapp, Miranda,* and *Fay.* Other opinions, such as *Argersinger* and *Morrissey,* clearly look toward further extension of constitutional guarantees. Moreover, in several cases, the prospect of future rejection of Warren Court decisions has been stressed primarily by dissents, usually by Justice Brennan, predicting the Court's eventual expansion of a minor exception to a Warren Court ruling into a total rejection of the earlier precedent. Civil libertarians and lower courts must recognize that Justice Brennan's cries of "wolf" have come forth so frequently that some Justices in the majority apparently have decided simply to ignore them. The absence of a response does not necessarily mean that Justice Brennan is accurately predicting the majority's intentions.

Of course, while the style of the Burger Court opinions on the whole is not negative, it also is not very positive. Opinions that openly balance interests on both sides and rely upon multifaceted standards do not "glorify" individual rights or even boldly call to the public attention major civil liberties issues. In this respect, the Burger Court lags far behind the Warren Court. The Warren Court opinions brought to the attention of the American people the important lesson that the observance of procedural safeguards is a significant indicator of the strength of our liberty. They spoke clearly and strongly on the need to keep law enforcement itself under the rule of law. As a result, the legitimacy of law enforcement practices became a subject of public debate rather than a concern only to the readers of *Commentary* or *Harpers*.

The Burger Court opinions, while obviously less helpful from the viewpoint of civil libertarians, still are not without potential value for their cause. Today, the public appears to be far more concerned about controlling crime than protecting the rights of suspects. Polls suggest that many people favor measures designed to "crack down" on crime, including some measures that would limit the rights of the accused. The Burger Court opinions suggesting possible future restrictions of *Mapp* or *Miranda* have been used by supporters of such conservative measures to promote their public acceptance. But neither the record of the Court nor the tenor of its majority opinions, taken as a whole, really supports a broad movement towards restricting the protections afforded the accused. Many civil libertarians might be well advised to examine the current Court's record carefully and to push aside the fact that Richard Nixon appointed four members of the current court. If they did so, they might find that their true interests lie in dropping their wholesale attacks on the Burger Court and in attempting instead to attract public attention to the various decisions of that Court that stress the continuing need to safeguard the basic rights of the accused.

Part Three CIVIL RIGHTS

CHAPTER 6   # "Forum: Equal Protection and the Burger Court"*

JESSE CHOPER, RAY FORRESTER***,
GERALD GUNTHER**** and PHILIP KURLAND*******

Professor Israel repeatedly emphasized in the preceeding article how the Burger Court, at least in the sphere of criminal rights has surprised those who too quickly and too boldly predicted what a Nixon Court was likely to do to the rights of the accused. Indeed, it was perhaps in the very nature of a "strict constructionist" Court to prove wrong anyone expecting great changes.

The Court's record on equal protection, however, has been much different. Its decisions on busing, affirmative action, and sex discrimination are hard to fit under the rubric of "strict constructionism." But if not "strict constructionist," what are they?

Five distinguished law professors try to sort out some of the questions raised by these decisions in the following article. Their comments are very much influenced by an article by Professor Gerald Gunther ("Forward: In Search of Evolving Doctrine on a Changing Court: A Model for a Newer Equal Protection," 86 *Harvard Law Review* (1972), p. 1) which presented a theoretical basis for much of what the Burger Court has done in the area of equal protection.

---

*Copyright © 1975 *Hastings Constitutional Law Quarterly*. Reprinted with permission and without footnotes and questions from 2 *Hastings Constitutional Law Quarterly* (1975), pp. 645-680.
  **Professor of Law, Boalt Hall School of Law
 ***Professor of Law, Cornell Law School
****Professor of Law, Stanford Law School
*****Professor of Law, University of Chicago Law School

At the invitation of the Quarterly, Professors Jesse Choper of Boalt Hall, Ray Forrester of Cornell, Gerald Gunther of Stanford and Philip Kurland of Chicago participated on March 22, 1975, in a panel discussion of recent events in equal protection cases. Professor Sullivan of Hastings College served as the moderator. A video-tape recording of the conversation is on reserve at the Prosser Videotape Library at Hastings.

Following initial remarks, members of the audience submitted written questions or asked questions orally of the panel. The following is a partially edited transcript of the two hour forum.

PROFESSOR FORRESTER: Thank you, Professor Sullivan. It's a pleasure to be here and to see so many good friends.

I would like to say initially that the subject we are discussing involves a great mass of material. A surprising number of recent cases have centered in one way or the other on this general matter. In attempting to review and simplify that material in these introductory remarks, I am cautioned by H.L. Mencken's observation that there is a simple answer to every complex problem, and it is wrong.

Although there is only one brief equal protection clause in the Constitution, the Supreme Court has managed to build it into a monolithic body of law, which is somewhat remindful of Mark Twain's description of the massive prehistoric animal which he saw in an exhibit at the Smithsonian. Back home someone asked, "What did you think about it, Sam?" and he replied, "One bone and a ton of plaster." But the ton of judicial plaster that has been fashioned around the equal protection clause has been reduced in recent years to two general doctrines—the traditional standard of equal protection and the so-called new standard of equal protection. For many years, as I see it, the new equal protection standard was not formalized. Comments are to be found using the words of the standard in early cases, such as the *McLaughlin* case and the *Skinner* case, but there was no definitive and doctrinal statement of it. However in 1969 in *Shapiro v. Thompson*, Justice Brennan's majority opinion stated the doctrine as if it were a general proposition of law and not something used *in arguendo* in deciding whether a particular situation offended the equal protection clause.

In 1973 Mr. Justice Powell, in *San Antonio Independent School District v. Rodriguez*, took the trouble, for the benefit of first-year law students and their law professors, to spell out the details of the new equal protection standard. When spelled out the rules became rather numerous. He said that the new test provides that when governmental action creates a class based on suspect criteria, or which abridges a fundamental right, it is subject to strict scrutiny by the judiciary, and the government has the heavy burden of showing to the satisfaction of the judges that there is a compelling governmental interest in making the classification. Further, the law must be structured with precision and tailored narrowly to serve legitimate objectives. It must choose the least drastic means, the least restrictive alternative to accomplish its ends, and the usual presumption of constitutionality is removed. In addition, Powell spelled out the traditional indicia of the suspectness of a class. The indicia are—whether the class is saddled with such disabilities, or subjected to such a history of purposeful or unequal treatment, or relegated to such a position of political powerlessness as to command extraordinary protection from the majoritarian political process.

He suggested that the answer to whether a particular subject involves a fundamental right lies in assessing whether there is such a right explicitly or implicitly guaranteed by the Constitution. Examples of the so-called suspect class are race, nationality and alienage. An example of a classification relating to a fundamental right is the right to travel, which was the basis for the *Shapiro* decision. These are, as I see it, the fundamental rules of the new equal protection doctrine.

I have had more difficulty in identifying precisely the traditional standard of equal protection. I find in my reading that there are a number of standards which come under this title. For example, Powell, in this same *Rodriguez* case has stated that the test is whether the state law bears some rational relationship to legitimate state purposes, but in the very same opinion he expressed it somewhat differently. He said the test is whether the law rationally *furthers* a legitimate state purpose. Chief Justice Warren, in the well-known *McGowan* case, frequently cited as the basic decision defining the traditional doctrine, made the statement: "Although no precise formula has been developed, a statutory discrimination will not be set aside if *any* state of facts reasonably may be conceived to justify it." Other judges in other cases have used different formulations. For example, Justice Harlan at one time said the test is whether the law is "rationally related to a legitimate governmental objective." Stewart, in the recent *Geduldig* case, said that the test is whether the line drawn by the state amounts to invidious discrimination. And in the 1974 case of *Kahn v. Shevin*, regarding sex discrimination, Justice Douglas used as the traditional test language to the effect that the law must be reasonably designed to further a valid state policy. But Mr. Justice Black, some years ago in the *Harper* case, pretty well spilled the beans by saying that the test really involves a number of catchwords such as "irrational," "unreasonable," "arbitrary," "invidious."

Now, in my view, these various verbalizations of the doctrine are not the same. As I see it, "*any* relation" is not the same as "*some* relation," or the same as "*a* relation," or as "*a reasonable* relation."

In addition to these varying formulations of the traditional test, the Court has recently been borrowing from the substantive due process doctrine in spelling out the meaning of the phrase. For example, in *Reed v. Reed*, Chief Justice Burger for the Court struck down a sex classification saying that the classification must rest on some ground of distinction having a "*fair* and *substantial* relation" to the object of the legislation, so that all persons in similar situations shall be treated alike. This language, "fair and substantial relation," is very similar to that used in one of the early and leading cases on substantive due process. In *Mugler v. Kansas,* which was decided in 1887, the opinion said the courts "are under a solemn duty to look at the substance of things . . . If, therefore, a statute purporting . . . to protect the public health . . . has no real or substantial relation to those objects . . . it is the duty of the courts to so adjudge . . ."

Thus, it seems we find the Court beginning to borrow from the concepts of substantive due process in spelling out the meaning of the equal protection clause.

Along with these two basic approaches, an additional development has taken place. It is illustrated by *Frontiero v. Richardson,* a 1973 sex discrimination case in which the Supreme Court held a federal statute unconstitutional. The Court couldn't use the equal protection clause to strike down the law because, as you know, that's in the Fourteenth Amendment and is applicable only to the states. It has no application to the federal government. So, the Court used the due process clause of the Fifth Amendment but borrowed and applied the specific rules of the new equal protection standard, such as the compelling state interest language, strict scrutiny, suspectness, fundamental rights, etc. This case, along with *Richardson v. Belcher* and *Roe v. Wade,* the abortion case, exemplifies the interchange of standards now practiced by the Court in the use of the due process and equal protection clauses of the Constitution. Now think of that combination. If there are two semantic blanks in the American Constitution which can mean anything you want them to mean if you have a vote on the Supreme Court, they are the due process clause and the equal protection clause. Holmes said, "Due process is reasonableness judicially determined." It appears now that equal protection is also reasonableness judicially determined. This, it seems to me, is significant in connection with the present status of the law and what is now going on within the Supreme Court. This is a guess, and I may be totally wrong, but it looks to me as if some of the members of the Court, when confronted with this combination of due process and equal protection under these highly restrictive interventionist standards, began to shy away from the use of the new doctrine in a categorical, comprehensive fashion in relation to additional subjects such as sex discrimination, poverty, and so on. And it seems that between 1969, when *Shapiro* first formally and explicitly asserted the doctrine, and the present time, something took place inside the Court. Some of the judges became concerned with the expansion of a doctrine that promised to establish a new and greater level of judicial power than had existed before. And subsequently, today we find that the momentum which appeared to be building with *Shapiro* toward a higher standard of judicial review through the extension of the new equal protection rules seems to have subsided.

The Court appears now to be marking time, deciding cases under other concepts which can gain the support of a majority of the Court. For example, in 1973 in *Vlandis v. Kline,* it used the rule against arbitrary irrebuttable presumptions to knock out a classification which could have been tested under the new equal protection docrine if the Court had chosen to use it. And the Court has also relied on the traditional equal protection standard more frequently. For example, Mr. Justice Douglas, in the recent 1974 case of *Kahn v. Shevin,* used traditional equal protection as the test to measure the constitutionality of a Florida law which gave a property tax exemption to widows but not to widowers. In the course of his opinion, he took occasion to observe, "The dissent would use the equal protection laws as a vehicle for reinstating notions of substantive due process that have been repudiated. 'We have returned to the original constitutional proposition that courts do not substitute their social and economical beliefs for the judgment of legislative bodies who are elected to pass laws.' " And he quoted the opinion of his colleague, Hugo Black, in the earlier case of *Ferguson v. Skrupa,* in which Black soundly condemned the doctrine of substantive due process and urged that it be abandoned.

I think that it is significant that Mr. Justice Douglas, who is sensitive to discrimination, would shy away, as I am suggesting, from the new equal protection doctrine in testing a law involving sex discrimination. His objection to the reinstatement of substantive due process through the equal protection law makes me think that he and other members of the Court have decided that the Court must not go too far in the use of the new equal protection tests. There is at least one member of the Court, however, who holds resolutely to the idea. Mr. Justice Brennan, who is primarily responsible for the effort to establish the new concept, continues to press the point, still uses it in his opinions, sometimes now in his dissenting opinions, and serves to remind the Court that the doctrine is still there. It has not been repudiated, though it seems to be used now in a more selective way than Brennan would prefer. The majority has not challenged the suspectness of race, they have not repudiated the fundamental nature of the right to travel. These still stand, but the majority refuses to move boldly into a new level of judicial review under the banner of new equal protection. Now the old doctrine, of course, is very lenient. It is permissive. In some of its forms such as the "any relation" test it is highly permissive. On its face it does not give the Court much power. It is a model expression of judicial self-restraint. On the other hand, the tests of new equal protection are highly interventionist, very strict. In fact, as Professor Gunther has pointed out in his Foreword, when the Court applies that test to a law, the result is nearly always fatal to the law. So, you have a hard choice there between the too permissive rule of the old test and the too restrictive and interventionist nature of the new test. We should pause here to give Professor Gunther credit for being the first, or one of the first scholars, who early on saw the implications here.

It has been suggested that the Court is formulating a third rule, the newer equal protection standard, by invoking the *real and substantial* relations test, which is a middle position between the old and the new and is designed to take care of those cases where the Court wants to strike down the law but does not find either of the two categories quite appropriate.

My own impression is that the Court is reaching "middle" results but without, so far, actually adopting a newer equal protection standard of moderate impact. So, it looks to me as if the Court is reaching the results it wants—middle results, more interventionist than the old test, but less restrictive than the new. It usually does this within the rubric of traditional equal protection language, borrowing at times from the language of substantive due process as in *Reed v. Reed.*

Well, like most law professors, I can go on forever on my favorite subject, but I am going to bring myself to stop—now!

PROFESSOR SULLIVAN: Professor Choper, would you like to speak at this time— either an initial statement or a comment on what Professor Forrester had to say?

PROFESSOR CHOPER: I would like to say at the outset that I am also very pleased to have been able to come across the bay this morning. I had intended to say, "to visit at a sister law school"; but given the subject of the discussion today, I think I better not say that for fear that since it is clear that the Hastings College of Law is subject to the state action prohibition of the Fourteenth Amendment, even under the narrowest reading, I would likely get in trouble.

I think it's fairly easy to state where the Court is and what it is doing so far as equal protection is concerned. If it finds a statutory classification that it feels is so bad that it ought to hold it unconstitutional, it does so. With increasing frequency it uses the traditional equal protection test in the process, finding statutory classifications either "arbitrary" or "irrational." On other occasions, it uses the "compelling state interest" test to invalidate a statutory classification. And, in several instances, when some doctrine or one case or another stands in the way, it uses the "irrebuttable presumption" approach to strike down a statutory classification.

On the other hand, when it believes that a particular classification is not so bad as to be held unconstitutional, it upholds it, usually invoking the rationality doctrine. It is very much like Thomas Reed Powell's classic description of the validity of state regulations of interstate commerce—but the results don't turn as much on who the members of the Court happen to be at a particular time but rather on what the feelings of a majority of the justices happen to be in respect to a particular classification.

Equal protection doctrine is many faceted. One can attempt to divide it in a number of ways. There is the category of classifications that impinge on "fundamental rights" and its companion category of classifications in respect to "suspect" groups. There is the "rationality" test on the one hand and the "compelling state interest" test on the other. Further, there is the distinction between *de jure* and *de facto* discriminations—an area that has been largely overlooked by the Court. We have heard very little from the Court in respect to this, although it hovers in the background very significantly as the Court expands the scope of the equal protection clause, especially in regard to suspect classifications. An important decision in this area that has generated surprisingly little attention is *Jefferson v. Hackney*. The Court was confronted with a *de facto* discrimination on the basis of race in the sense that the statute before it operated in a statistical fashion to discriminate against minority races. The case involved a fairly complicated Texas system of funding welfare programs. It was demonstrated to the Court, to put it generally, that the state more generously funded those public assistance programs that benefited groups with relatively small minority populations than it did those welfare programs whose recipients were more heavily black and chicano. The argument was that since the system operated to discriminate against minority groups, it ought to be judged by the strict equal protection standard of review. Yet in an opinion by Mr. Justice Rehnquist, with no real dissent from the basic proposition, the Court held that so long as there was a rational basis for the state's classification, it would survive equal protection attack.

Another highly important aspect of equal protection doctrine on which the Court seems to have carefully avoided making any significant statement concerns "benign" or "reverse" discrimination. So far as race is concerned, the Court totally sidestepped the problem in the *De Funis* case. In two sex discrimination cases, the Court upheld such a classification: *Kahn v. Shevin,* involving a discrimination against widowers in the grant of property tax exemptions; *Schlesinger v. Ballard,* involving a discrimination against male naval officers in the matter of mandatory discharges. In both of these cases the Court used the rationality test, and it is very difficult to distinguish these cases from those in which it has used this very same test to invalidate discriminations against women.

This leads to the last matter I would like to comment on for just a few minutes—the tremendous ambiguity that exists with respect to suspect classifications, that aspect of equal protection, so far as the Burger Court is concerned, that appears to be the most fruitful area for expansion.

The Court under Chief Justice Burger has certainly not retreated to any meaningful degree from the notion that discriminations against racial minorities are suspect. It has also made clear what was unclear before the Burger Court—that discriminations against aliens are also to be treated as suspect. This means that almost all discriminations against aliens are going to be held invalid. I say "almost all" because the Court has left open the issue of those particular kinds of state discriminations against aliens that deal with matters peculiar to citizenship such as voting and holding high public office. Beyond this, the Court has also left open the very interesting question of federal discriminations against aliens, that is, whether the national government's very broad power over immigration and naturalization granted in Article I will result in the Court applying a different equal protection standard for discriminations imposed by the federal government as opposed to those imposed by the states. That would probably be about the only area of equal protection adjudication in which the Court is going to treat federal discriminations differently from those by the states.

But when one looks beyond race and alienage at the opinions of the Burger Court, there is substantial ambiguity and confusion. The sex discrimination cases are illustrative. In the past several years, the Court has struck down two statutory discriminations against women—*Reed v. Reed* and *Frontiero v. Richardson*. Both decisions used the rationality test despite the fact, I think, that by any reasonable standard the statutory classifications were perfectly rational in accomplishing a permissible government purpose. On the other hand, when the Court was confronted, in *Geduldig v. Aiello,* with a statutory classification that looked as though it were a discrimination against women—a California statute that denied disability insurance benefits for pregnancy—the Court held it to be not violative of equal protection because it was not sex discrimination.

Geduldig raises some fascinating issues as to how discrimination is to be defined. Nonetheless, it is pretty difficult, I believe, to justify the Court's conclusion that when a particular trait that is common exclusively to only one of the sexes is involved, that that is not sex discrimination. At the same time, when confronted with statutory discriminations in favor of women, the Court has had little difficulty using the rationality standard to uphold those classifications.

So, I think that we still don't know precisely where the Court is so far as sex discrimination is concerned. The record is far from clear that the Court is willing to strike down every form of sex discrimination, even those against women, as is evidenced by the *Geduldig* case. Nor is it wholly clear that the Court will uphold every discrimination in favor of women. But there is no doubt that a majority of the Court has been unwilling to go one inch beyond the rationality test, despite the fact that its use in this area involves a good deal of waffling and fudging.

The other two major classifications that advocates have put forward as being suspect are illegitimacy and poverty. Again, it is very difficult to make any doctrinal sense out of what the Court has done. In *Weber v. Aetna Casualty and Surety Co.* it came very close to holding that illegitimacy was a suspect classification. But Mr. Justice Powell writing for the Court managed at the very end of the opinion, in striking down a state discrimination against illegitimate children, to say that the state interest was neither compelling nor rational and thus couldn't be upheld under any circumstances.

Last term, in *Jimenez v. Weinberger,* the Court speaking through Chief Justice Burger was careful to point out that it had not decided whether illegitimacy was a suspect classification. The *Jimenez* case has drawn little attention. But the doctrinal approach, particularly coming from Chief Justice Burger, is absolutely fascinating. The chief justice, who has consistently berated his colleagues for using the irrebuttable presumption notion in a series of cases under the patina of the due process clause, then used it himself in the *Jimenez* case, but this time in the process of finding a violation of equal protection.

Finally, the poverty classification seems to me to be one that also manifests the ambiguity of the Burger Court in the matter of equal protection. I guess that it was widely believed that if the suspect classification category were going to be expanded, a *de jure* discrimination against poor people, that is, the state singling out poor people for adverse treatment, would easily qualify. I think that if one went through the statute books of the fifty states and of the United States Code, one would find very, very few such laws that explicitly discriminate against poor people. Yet when one came to the Court's attention, the Court managed to uphold it. *James v. Valtierra* was a case involving a California constitutional provision which required that, in order to have low-cost housing built in any particular area, a special hurdle had to be overcome—it had to be approved by referendum. The Court found no violation of equal protection, saying that there was no explicit discrimination against poor people but in a way which, I think, just will not withstand analysis.

On the other hand, the Court has in a number of decisions struck down *de facto* discriminations against poor people. It seemed in the first years of the Burger Court that that was going to be an area of potential expansion. There were three cases—*Williams v. Illinois, Tate v. Short* and *Boddie v. Connecticut*—in which the Court invalidated *de facto* discriminations against poor people. *Williams* and *Tate* rested on equal protection; the *Boddie* decision went on due process grounds because Mr. Justice Harlan wrote for the Court. *Williams* and *Tate* involved the question of indigents having to go to jail after a criminal conviction because they were unable to pay the fine. The Court, following the decisions of its predecessor in *Griffin v. Illinois* and *Douglas v. California,* held that it was violative of equal protection to discriminate against poor people in this way. Although using the due process clause in *Boddie,* but effectively following the earlier view of the equal protection cases, the Court struck down a requirement that persons pay filing fees in order to obtain a divorce. Note that none of these were statutory classifications that explicitly singled out poor people for adverse treatment. They simply operated adversely as far as poor people were concerned. Yet the trend was halted in the case of *United States v. Kras,* when the Court held that equal protection did not require the government to waive the fee for an indigent in order to become bankrupt. And the same result was reached in *Ortwein v. Schwab* in respect to a fee in order to get judicial review of adverse welfare decisions, the Court holding that this *de facto* discrimination against poor people was not violative of equal protection.

Overall, poor people have fared better than racial minorities so far as *de facto* discriminations are concerned. But in the one case involving an explicit discrimination against the poor, *James v. Valtierra,* the Court was unwilling to find an equal protection violation. Thus, this series of decisions dealing with suspect classifications illustrates the proposition, I think, that one cannot discern or predict any really meaningful doctrine, so far as the Court's equal protection decisions go.

I will stop there.

PROFESSOR SULLIVAN: Thank you. Mr. Gunther, it's your turn.

PROFESSOR GUNTHER: Well, I think enough has already been said to indicate that a group of law professors getting together to talk about equal protection may give constitutional law a bad name. I think it is clear that no one here has a magic wand to straighten out what continues to be the most chaotic, least thoughtfully considered, and least adequately justified area of constitutional law.

I suppose one can say that at the end of the Warren era doctrine was a good deal clearer, though in large part unjustified. What the Warren Court did, as Professor Forrester has said, was increasingly to expand strict scrutiny of suspect classifications without explaining how it got there. Moreover, the Court developed or suggested a whole range of fundamental interests which triggered strict scrutiny. Very often, there was indeed clarity, but also lack of proffered justification.

The appeal of the equal protection clause to the Warren Court was evident. I think it was a two-fold appeal. Partly, the appeal lay in the fact that equal protection did not carry with it the bad reputation that substantive due process had. Of course, no good, modern, liberal justice would openly engage in substantive due process adjudication. Equal protection was a fairly inert and harmless looking doctrine, a doctrine which did not carry a great deal of baggage—baggage of disreputable history. The second appeal was obviously the appeal of egalitarianism and equality. As Mr. Kurland long ago pointed out, it was a great banner to carry, although a most difficult one to apply, for equalizing across the board was neither historically nor constitutionally justifiable. Nor was it anything any rational Court would try to do in terms of eliminating all classifications, or all differential impacts of legislation, or all differentials in society. So, by the end of the Warren Court we knew roughly where we were, though not why, and not where else we might be going. Most of us were uncertain about what new interests might be included within the purview of the new equal protection, by analogy to other interests which were regarded as fundamental. And it was hard to explain how the Court got to new suspect classifications and fundamental interests once it went beyond the obvious area of race discrimination. But all observers knew very well that if they could not persuade the Court to discover a trigger for strict scrutiny, their cause was hopeless. The deferential attitude was about as harmless to challenged legislation as the strict scrutiny attitude was a guarantee that the law would be held invalid.

Well, what has happened with the Burger Court? The Burger Court is less predictable. The Burger Court is a lot less clear in its doctrine. The Burger Court has not done much better than the Warren Court in justifying what interventions it has undertaken. My attempted argument of a couple of years ago was not that the Burger Court had made sense but that some of its steps might be explained in a way which would make some sense if the Court were willing to articulate the reasons and apply the standards consistently. The one thing that one can say about the Burger Court's performance in equal protection is that equal protection has remained an interventionist tool. That, I suppose, is a reflection of the phenomenon that people putting on those black robes and sitting in Washington—no matter how anti-interventionist they may be in theory and how strict constructionist they may be in profession—cannot resist the temptation to contribute their two cents to a lot of issues that grab their attention. I don't think that is a bad thing. I think the Constitution justifiably warrants some intervention. The real question is: What are *adequate* justifications for the intervention?

The phenomenon that I commented on in my article, as Mr. Forrester mentioned earlier, is that the minimal rationality standard—which had been a very deferential standard in the Warren years, and which was equivalent to saying that if a case fell into that deferential area of the old equal protection, the law would be sustained—that standard has in the 1970's become a basis for intervention. Recognizing the difficulties of model building and simplifying, I nevertheless tried to argue that the Warren Court had been too deferential in applying the old equal protection, rationality standard. I did not try to set up in my simple model a third layer of intermediate scrutiny. Rather, I suggested some closing of the gap between strict scrutiny and deferential scrutiny (or non-scrutiny). I argued that the Court could justifiably examine, with some genuine scrutiny, legislation even if it did not involve a suspect classification or impinge on a fundamental interest or right. (The latter, of course, hardly needed the equal protection clause to justify strict scrutiny.) In that area of rationality review, I urged that the Court could do more by bending over backwards less, by not hypothesizing conceivable purposes. I argued, for example, that classifications should be tested in terms of articulated or actual stated purposes, instead of testing the necessary "fit" in terms of purposes the Court's imaginativeness had supplied. That search for purposes is a thorny area which we can come back to.

The more difficult, second part of my appeal is that, instead of simply saying "a reasonable man *could* conceive of a connection" between means and ends, the Court would exercise a real, though modest, scrutiny of the relationship between means and ends. In short, the Court would test in terms of articulated rather than hypothesized purposes, and it would ask whether the means truly did, within some area of permissible flexibility promote those ends.

Now you are quite right, Professor Forrester, that the Court has not written an opinion saying "that's the new test." I should add that when I wrote the Foreword, it was the first term the Court had really significantly struck down laws while invoking the old rationality standard; and I did not find a single case among the half dozen examples of that year that satisfied my model. I said in effect that genuinely all of the cases that I found which invalidated on the basis of the rationality test were in fact Mickey Mouse cases. They were cases where the Court had to some extent fudged; it had applied greater scrutiny than it asserted, and it had presumably done so on the basis of perceived but unarticulated values.

In short, the cases on which I built my model were not nearly as value-free as the Court's opinions suggested. Now one conclusion that one can draw from that is that rationality review is bound to be a hopeless effort, inevitably a facade for obscuring interventionism. The conclusion which I tried to draw, perhaps in naive optimism, was that though those cases did not do the job right, the justices could do something sensible by taking seriously what they were saying as to standards in those cases.

What has happened since then, and one can count heads, is that just about everybody on the Court has now written an opinion at one time or another which uses significant ingredients of something similar to my argument. There are sometimes examples in Powell opinions, and Brennan ones, and others. Justice Brennan's dissent in *Schlesinger v. Ballard* last fall is among the examples. There are others refusing to hypothesize purposes and insisting on finding a substantial connection between means and ends. The Court, however, has not done it consistently, or even with adequate explicit care—except perhaps *Wiesenfeld* this week. You can count heads, however, and find considerable support: Brennan and others especially in dissent; Powell in several concurrences, as well as dicta in majority opinions, as in *McGinnis v. Royster*. The majority has used it in some cases, in effect, without articulation.

Though the Court has not come to grips with it as a generalized theory, in particular cases it is very useful to litigants. The most recent case, *Weinberger v. Wiesenfeld,* is in a sense very much like that. It was a sex discrimination case, and it was argued very much along newer equal protection grounds. Women's rights advocate Professor Ruth Bader Ginsburg of Columbia had originally submitted a long brief in *Reed v. Reed* arguing that sex should be a suspect classification. Those fifty-some pages of fine argument got nowhere with the Court. The Court struck down that law on what purported to be a rationality standard, which I do not think could be explained without some special sensitivity to sex classifications which they were unwilling to avow.

In cases since, the arguments for sex as a suspect classification have understandably become weaker and have been diminished; and the arguments against particular types of legislation have emphasized lack of connection between means and articulated ends. Again, some of those cases cannot be explained in terms of the formulas used. I suppose *Weinberger v. Wiesenfeld,* of last Wednesday, may come closest of all the decisions so far to applying the "newer equal protection" in a straightforward, genuine way, without hidden factors inducing an actual scrutiny more intense than the asserted one. It is interesting that eight people on the Court, everyone that voted, with Justices Powell and Rehnquist writing separate concurrences, all went along with the basic approach of Justice Brennan's majority opinion, an opinion which is simply an examination of the legislative purpose as it appears from the legislative history and the face of the statute. It is unwilling to hypothesize other purposes or to accept alleged purposes without basis in the record. And having discovered the actual or articulated legislative purposes, the Court asks: Does the gender-based classification in this case make any contribution to furthering those purposes? The Court refuses to find other conceivable purposes, limits itself to the actual purposes that came out of the legislative history, and finds those purposes not significantly furthered by this classification. And, happily, they then strike down the classification. And rightly so, I believe, and in accordance with the model I tried to set forth. There are a few cases similar to that. But—unfortunately, I think, for the future of "newer equal protection"—this variety of interventionism is not yet an across-the-board phenomenon. So far, the minimal-rationality-with-bite approach is being applied in an ad hoc manner.

I think that what we have is a group of justices who can't resist intervening sometimes; by an large, a new group of justices who have not yet developed an adequate feel for connecting one case in one area with another. They respond to situations in terms of particularized contexts. "Newer equal protection" is a convenient test to invoke occasionally during this groping, searching period. It at least makes a little bit more sense than the nonsense of the irrebuttable presumptions analysis, which is essentially equal protection analysis under a completely misleading name. But the "newer equal protection" won't be respectable and truly defensible unless and until it is taken more seriously as a generally applicable rule.

I suppose that I am less hopeful now than I was two years ago that the Court will come up with a more coherent explanation of what they are doing, with consistent applications. I recognize more difficulties now than I spoke about in the Foreword, as to both purposes and means, and in application. I would hate to be trying to decide some of the cases which would be thrown at me to decide. My continued, limited optimism comes from the fact that the sheer accumulation of cases is such that there may be some institutional pressure to try and sit back, particularly as justices get more experienced, to try and make more coherent sense out of this. I think it is possible to make some sense out of it. It is not offered to us by the Court today. It is ironic that Chief Justice Burger is the one who talks most often, going around the country, telling everybody that the courts are getting flooded by too much litigation. I can't imagine a more flooding device than to be as erratic and ad hoc-ish as this Court is being in the use of equal protection. Why shouldn't one file a suit in terms of the lack of ends-means connections, as well as the other debris that floats around the books, to see if one can win? It is not exactly a litigation-stifling device. On the other hand, I do not expect that Court to agree to what Justice Rehnquist's position was at one time: to have broad deferential attitudes everywhere outside the race area. It is interesting that Justice Rehnquist, for the first time as far as I know, concurs in *Wiesenfeld* and finds a constitutionally inadequate connection between means and ends in an equal protection case. So, he too has joined the team outside of the race area to find equal protection an interventionist device, sometimes. How much is "sometimes" and where is "sometimes" is beyond the scope of this discussion. I hope.

PROFESSOR SULLIVAN: Professor Kurland will now have his opportunity to either support or demolish the statements which have previously been made.

PROFESSOR KURLAND: I am not going to do either.

It is quite clear to me, and I expect to you, that there is not much left to be said on the subject. But I haven't come all this distance to sit here in silence or merely for the purpose of enjoying this climate.

Mr. Gunther, at the close of his remarks, made a statement reminiscent of Thomas Reed Powell's brief restatement of the commerce clause of the Constitution, which, as I recall, was that the federal government may regulate interstate commerce. Part two was that state government may also regulate interstate commerce, but not too much. How much is too much, he added, was beyond the scope of this restatment.

My own preference for epitome of the Court's equal protection cases would be a scene in Hamlet, in which he is walking on stage and reading a book. Asked what it is that he is reading, he said, "Words, my lord, words." And I think that is what the problem is with the so-called doctrines of the equal protection clause. They are only words.

We talk about doctrines as if they were realities, but I think that by now you have learned that there is very little, if any, substance to the so-called doctrines of the equal protection clause, whether it be the "new equal protection" or the "old equal protection." For me it is quite clear. The new equal protection, like the old equal protection, is the old substantive due process. This means, as pointed out to you already, that the Court will undertake to tell the state and federal legislatures when they have gone beyond the bounds of what the Supreme Court thinks it is appropriate for them to do. The difference between the new equal protection and the old substantive due process is essentially the difference in the hierarchy of values of the Court.

The even older equal protection clause paralleled the old due process clause. That is, there was a subordination to the legislative will, which, I think, was what was orginally contemplated by those who framed the Fourteenth Amendment. I must say it is within these terms that Mr. Gunther's third doctrine could become viable. If it is going to become viable at all, it is concerned with means and not ends.

In short, there are a lot of rationalizations provided by law professors indirectly, and immediately by law clerks, who submit these lengthy dissertations to their justices for their signatures and dissemination as the wisdom of the highest court of the land.

I have really only one or two points to make that may not yet have been made here. One that I think is of some importance is to recognize that the language of "strict scrutiny," the language of the so-called new equal protection clause, is derived essentially from the First Amendment cases; the First Amendment cases in which the argument was made by Mr. Justice Black and by others for the "first-ness" of the First Amendment. It is this language of legislative presumption that you find floating through the opinions of the Court now dealing with equal protection rather than the First Amendment. The same kinds of burdens on the states, the same kinds of judicial limitations on exercise of state powers, are found in the equal protection area that once were the concern of the First Amendment area.

The second point is that both in the First Amendment area and in the equal protection area the Court speaks in terms of irrebuttable or unrebuttable presumptions. The essence of most of these cases is to be found in allocating the burden of proof or the burden of persuasion. With the assignment of the burden of persuasion you achieve a resolution of the outcome of the controversy, as those who are sophisticated about the practice of law have understood for a long time. One might say he doesn't care what the rule is, so long as he can assign the burden of proof. Once having assigned the burden of proof, it is very easy to say that, to hold that, it has not been carried.

Let me say third, and last, that we seem to have evaded, up until this point—because it is an almost impossible problem for resolution—what do we mean by equal protection, or more clearly, what do we mean by equality? Here, one might take notice of the fact that in the equal protection clause the Constitution uses the word "equal" as an adjective. It speaks, I like to think, of a requirement of equality of treatment. When we talk about equality as if it were the same thing as equal protection, however, we tend more to be talking about equality of condition. Equal protection has become a noun and is no longer an adjective. And it is never clear to the justices or those who read the justices' opinions whether the question they are talking about is equality of condition or equality of treatment. It is quite clear to many of the professional commentators that what they are seeking is equality of condition. For them the equal protection clause is the only vehicle: it permits equality of conditions to be imposed by the judiciary. And that is one of the reasons there is such strong support in the academic writing for the equal protection opinions of the Supreme Court.

PROFESSOR CHOPER: I would add one or two points. First, I totally agree with the view that many of the developments in equal protection litigation have been nothing more than the old substantive due process. And I think it is important to recognize that, in addition, the irrebuttable presumption device is also nothing more than substantive due process. So, too, has been the Burger Court's expansion of the notion that constitutional rights exist even though nowhere mentioned in the Constitution, a notion most notably put forward in the abortion cases.

Now it is also true that by the end of the era of the Warren Court there had been a series of cases which could also be subject to this description. But whether one wants to be critical of the results or not, the Warren Court decisions were quite straightforwardly stated, and they also were fairly limited. It's clear that the Court made a constitutional right out of the right to vote, although it did so under the aegis of the equal protection clause. Similarly, the Warren Court revived or re-created a constitutionally protected right to travel. And it may well have been that if the Warren Court had continued, a large number of other essentially substantive constitutional rights would have been developed, again under the aegis of the equal protection clause. But the decision in *Dandridge v. Williams,* in which the Court upheld the Maryland maximum welfare grant statute, seemed to put an end to the "fundamental rights" doctrine. If that had gone the other way, then it may well have presaged a significant expansion of "fundamental rights" under equal protection—in essence, substantive due process.

But I am not at all confident that there would have been a majority of the Warren Court at the end that would have come out differently in *Dandridge.* It is clear, for example, that Mr. Justice Black was not about to go that route, and there was a strong indication that the chief justice himself was not about to do so, as evidenced by his dissenting opinion in *Shapiro v. Thompson,* in which he argued that residency requirements for welfare did not violate equal protection. In any event, we know that the Burger Court formally called a halt to all of this in *Dandridge.* This was made even plainer in the school finance case from Texas in which the Court indicated that it would only occasionally hold a particular right to be protected by the Constitution and then subject any restriction of it to strict scrutiny when there was a classification made. Otherwise, the Burger Court said that it was at the end of the road in respect to "fundamental rights" and indeed there are some cases that bear that out.

But the fact is that it is only in *some* cases. Take the decision in *Village of Belle Terre v. Boraas* where the Court applied the most deferential rationality standard despite the fact that there were lurking rights that had been held protected under the Constitution. At least a reasonably respectable opinion could have been written coming out the other way in *Belle Terre.* But the Court simply stated that it was not going to apply strict scrutiny. On the other hand, they did apply strict scrutiny in *Eisenstadt v. Baird* without admitting it. They did it again in the food stamp case, *United States Department of Agriculture v. Moreno,* again without admitting it. They said that they struck the law down on grounds of irrationality, as they also said in *Lindsey v. Normet* when invalidating a double bond for appeal provision for tenants who had been evicted under the Oregon procedures.

While it may be that, in the main, what the Burger Court has done is not far different from what the Warren Court was doing, I think it is much less predictable and much less candid. Whether one agrees or disagrees with the direction that the Warren Court had taken, at least it was mainly done quite openly. I see Phil Kurland shaking his head and I am anxious to hear his comments on that, although I have seen some of them on occasion in the past. I believe that the Burger Court is less predicatable, more lacking in candor, and engaging in much more fudging and waffling.

PROFESSOR GUNTHER: I will register a partial dissent. I don't think the Warren Court was all that candid, but I leave that to Phil. As I said earlier, I do think the Burger Court is unpredictable. I think that some of your adjectives and nouns are a little harsh. I think one ought to distinguish among members of the Burger Court. I think some are trying harder and doing better at trying to come to grips with the legacy of doctrine and trying to build a new body than are others. Justice Powell is being more critical of some of the slipshod stuff that an occasional majority or plurality opinion comes up with, and he is not the only one who is trying more diligently to come up with coherent statements.

The emphasis on the similarity between the new equal protection and substantive due process is absolutely right. I think, however, that that risks losing sight of the fact that there is more to equal protection than the amorphous strands of the new equal protection.

The hostility to substantive due process was largely a hostility to the Supreme Court fishing out of thin air its own predilections with inadequate textual, structural and historical justification. It was hostility to the Court curtailing particular *ends* of legislation because they did not conform to particular values the majority had unjustifiably "discovered" as a brake on legislative objectives. But due process, as well as equal protection, has another significant ingredient—a focus on rationality of *means* rather than legitimacy of ends. At least one can state that means-ingredient distinguishably, although, I confess, the line between means and ends is hard to draw in practice.

The bad legacy of substantive due process and of ends-oriented equal protection involves a block to legislative ends, an imposition of judicial values as to objectives. That is something from which the Burger Court is overtly retreating— as to equal protection at least, though not as to due process, as *Roe v. Wade* shows. Ends scrutiny under equal protection was something the Warren Court was far more ready to do and often unjustifiably so in terms of the constitutional basis for it.

The other part of equal protection which I have focused on can be effective judicial scrutiny which does *not* by and large second-guess legislative ends and which simply puts some pressure on the political process to air more clearly just how its *means* contribute to the ends it has chosen to articulate. Now it is a thorny area as I have said, though I think it is quite doable. I agree that much of the purported means scrutiny of the Burger Court has been disguised ends scrutiny. I do not think I am persuaded that means scrutiny must always be a subterfuge for imposing hierarchies of values without saying so. I think there is —maybe very limited—but some remnant of a justifiable judicial role with respect to taking seriously a requirement the Court has stated all along: that there be some minimal rational relationship between means and ends.

What I tried to suggest in the Foreword—and what I think has been done by some justices, some lower courts, and occasionally the Supreme Court—is to try to exercise that rationality review of means fairly and with relative neutrality (if there can be such a thing as relative neutrality). Most of the sex discrimination cases do involve a hidden ingredient and degree of value preference, a sort of semi-suspect-ness of gender-based classifications without quite saying so. As I have said, I think *Weinberger v. Wiesenfeld* this week may be a case at last to illustrate the proper approach even where sex isn't involved. The *Wiesenfeld* Court goes through an exercise which is replicable in other areas as well, of simply asking quite honestly just what you can get out of the record as to legislative purposes, and asking whether the chosen means make any real contribution to the stated ends.

I think that the means ingredient of equal protection has a legitimacy of its own. It's full of problems, the biggest one no doubt that it risks use as a subterfuge for ends scrutiny under a different name. I do not think that we ought to give up on possible legitimate uses too quickly. After all, the Court purports to be doing it sometimes. And sometimes—more rarely—it even does so genuinely. I think one useful thing an academic may be able to do is keep yelling at the judges and their law clerks that they ought to try handling it more honestly, neutrally, generally and genuinely.

PROFESSOR KURLAND: I have just two remarks, if I may. The first is that the perfidy of the Warren Court is every bit as great as the perfidy of the Burger Court, and I am prepared to supply a bibliography on both subjects. I don't think I have been partial to one or the other. Thomas Reed Powell when introducing Mr. Chief Justice Stone at a law review banquet at Columbia, said he wanted to introduce a man who is neither parital on the one hand, nor impartial on the other. I think that the point made as to the lack of clarity or consistency of the Burger Court is well taken. But I think it's well taken essentially because there isn't a cohesive majority. It's easier to be consistent when you have a group of five, all of whom share a hierarchy of values, than when you have a Court which is essentially divided three, three, and three, and the three in the middle are not a cohesive group themselves. They just go to one side or the other depending on the issue involved. So, it is quite true that the Burger Court opinions in this area do not afford predictability. It's not, however, because of the statements of doctrine they contain, but because of the personal preferences of each of the jurists.

PROFESSOR FORRESTER: I would like to say that I am doubtful that the Warren Court, if it had continued would have extended the equal protection doctrine vigorously. In counting heads, Stewart, it seems relatively clear, has not fully embraced the substantive equal protection concept. His *Frontiero* concurring opinion is really the swing opinion which kept the Court from putting sex classifications into the suspect category. Douglas has declared his hesitation in the *Kahn* case. Warren, in the *Shapiro* case, indicated that he had doubt about the concept. Black, in the *Harper* case, clearly spelled out his repeated objection to such judicial intervention. Now that leaves Marshall, if you need five votes. Here, I would like to read a statement by Marshall which I think is significant and which may also describe the present status of the law in this field, or at least its actual result-oriented operation. In *Rodriguez,* he said,

> I must once more voice my disagreement with the Court's rigidified approach to equal protection analysis. [*Citations omitted.*] The Court apparently seeks to establish today that equal protection cases fall into one of two neat categories which dictate the appropriate standard of review—strict scrutiny or mere rationality. But this Court's decisions in the field of equal protection defy such easy categorization. A principled reading of what this Court has done reveals that it has applied a spectrum of standards in reviewing discrimination allegedly violative of the Equal Protection Clause. This spectrum clearly comprehends variations in the degree of care with which the Court will scrutinize particular classifications, depending, I believe, on the constitutional and societal importance of the interest adversely affected and the recognized invidiousness of the basis upon which the particular classification is drawn. I find in fact that many of the Court's recent decisions embody the very sort of reasoned approach to equal protection analysis for which I previously argued—that is, an approach in which "concentration [is] placed upon the character of the classification in question, the relative importance to the individuals in the class discriminated against of the governmental benefits that they do not receive, and the asserted state interests in support of the classification."

In other words, Marshall seems not to accept the new equal protection doctrine as such, but to look upon equal protection as another exercise in balancing and weighing, or the sifting of the facts and the weighing of the circumstances, as in the *Burton* case.

Counting these five heads makes me dubious whether the Warren Court would have gone forward more strongly than the Burger Court in pressing the new equal protection concept. Certainly, so far as the Burger Court is concerned, you can't find a more interventionist decision in the books than *Roe v. Wade,* whether you agree with it or not.

• • • • • •

CHAPTER 7   **"Some Post—*Bakke, Weber,* and *Fullilove* Reflections on 'Reverse Discrimination' "***

HENRY J. ABRAHAM*

Is the Burger Court conservative or liberal? One problem that plagues those who seek an answer to this question is that the terms, conservative and liberal, seem to have changed in meaning or, to put it possibly more accurately, to have had their meanings changed for them. To be a liberal in the fifties obviously meant opposition to the use of race as a means of distinguishing among individuals. To be a liberal in the eighties, however, means for many that race should be considered in deciding who should be admitted to professional schools and who should be hired.

Affirmative action or reverse discrimination—one's choice of terms reflects one's perception of the facts and one's likely conclusion from such facts—has not only triggered a sometimes painful examination of what it means to be liberal or conservative, but also what is judicial activism and what is judicial self-restraint.

Harvard Law Professor Archibald Cox, for example, has criticized the Court's decision in *California v. Bakke* (1978), striking down California-Davis's Medical School's special admissions program, for failing to show sufficient deference to the wishes of the California legislature. In contrast, Henry Abraham, Professor of Government at the University of Virginia seems to find little wrong with the Powell opinion in *Bakke* that so troubles Cox, but does find evidence of

*This article is a revision of an article that appeared originally in Volume 14 of *The University of Richmond Law Review* (1980), pp. 373-388. It is printed with the permission of the author and *The University of Richmond Law Review,* © 1979.
**James Hart Professor of Government and Foreign Affairs, University of Virginia

activism in *United Steel Workers v. Weber* (1979) where the Court upheld an agreement that reserved 50 percent of the openings in a craft
training program for blacks despite what Abraham sees as a clearly
contrary intent on the part of Congress in enacting Title VII of the
Civil Rights Act of 1964.

Though Professor Abraham's own opinions are expressed clearly
in the following article and his argumentation is most persuasive, the
reader is not likely to come to any easy conclusion concerning the
conservatism or liberalism, activism or self-restraint of the Burger
Court. In the area of affirmative action or reverse discrimination, as in
the other areas explored in this book, these terms seem less and less
helpful in understanding the Court and what it has done and is doing.

I.

So much has been said, written, and emoted concerning the subject of "reverse discrimination" that it represents a veritably frustrating experience to endeavor to come to grips with it in a non-redundant, non-banal, non-breast beating
manner. The difficulty is compounded by the all-too pervasive substitution of
passion for reason on that wrenching issue—one that, admittedly, invites passion.
Indeed, passion informed not an insignificant number of the record filings of the
120 briefs *amici curiae* in 1978 in the first central "reverse discrimination" case
of *Regents of the University of California v. Allan Bakke,* (438 U.S. 268), in which
oral argument had been presented to the Supreme Court of the United States in
mid-October 1977. It took place in a sardine-like packed Court chamber, with
more than 200 putative spectators waiting in line all night in the hope of perhaps
hearing one three-minute segment of that potential bellweather decision—toward
which the court, in an unusual action, called for the filing of supplementary briefs
by all parties concerned two weeks later in order to argue specifically the *statutory*
question(s), involved in the application of Title VI of the Civil Rights Act of 1964.
Passion similarly governed the denouement of the second major "reverse discrimination" case, *United Steel Workers and Kaiser Aluminum & Chemical Corporation
v. Weber,* (433 U.S. 193), which the Court decided in 1979, almost exactly one
year after the *Bakke* holdings, and that of the third, *Fullilove v. Klutznick,* (100
S.Ct. 2758), which followed again one year later, in 1980. And passion, however
comprehensive emotionally, has clouded the arguments and contentions of even
the most cerebral professional as well as lay observers of the "reverse discrimination" issue, the resolution of which may well constitute a watershed in this
particularly crucial aspect of the race syndrome, of what Gunnar Myrdal more
than three decades ago so pointedly titled an "American Dilemma." Indeed, a satisfactory resolution may never take place, given the Supreme Court's 1980-81 term

policy of ducking the issue by either affirming lower court rulings or refusing to grant review in cases designed to reach it for resolution.

In the hope of avoiding an abject surrender to the aforementioned passion(s), I shall do my best to discuss the matter on a rational basis while pledging to strive to eschew what Headmaster Stanley Bosworth of St. Anne's Episcopal School in Brooklyn so tellingly, if perhaps a mite expansively, identified as "the piety, puritanism, and guilt that have combined to stir the worst semantic confusion" conceivable in this emotion-charged policy spectrum. It would thus be helpful to try to identify at the outset what we are, or *should be*, talking about in any attempted analysis of the constellation of "reverse discrimination," and what we *should not be* talking about. To do that it is necessary to find what the concept *means.* "I only want to know what the words mean," once commented Mr. Justice Oliver Wendell Holmes, Jr., probably *the* judicial philosopher of our age; but he freely admitted, with E.M. Forster, that there is "wine in words." A lot of wine and other rather less consumable liquids have been poured into the notion, into the alleged meaning, of "reverse discrimination."

II.

Stipulating the audience of these ruminations to be educated, intelligent human beings, who read, see and/or hear the news that informs our *vie quotidienne,* I am comfortable in assuming a basic familiarity with the issues involved. I am also aware that and—I daresay, without exception—any listener or reader will have strong feelings on the matter. So do I. We would not be human if we did not; while they operate on a host of levels and are triggered at vastly diverse moments, we all have consciences. Stipulating these facets, I should first endeavor to make clear what "reverse discrimination" is *not*: (1) It is *not* action, be it in the governmental or private sector, designed to remedy the absence of proper and needed educational preparation or training by special, even if costly, primary and/or secondary school level preparatory programs or occupational skill development, such as "Head Start," "Upward Bound," etc., always provided that access to these programs is not bottomed on race but on education, and/or economic need, be it cerebral or manual. (2) It is *not* the utilization of special classes or supplemental tutoring or training, regardless of the costs involved (assuming, of course, that these have been properly authorized and appropriated) on any level of the educational or training process, from the very pre-nursery school bottom to the very top of the professional training ladder. (3) It is of course *not* the scrupulous exhortation and enforcement of absolute standards of non-discrimination on the basis of race, sex, religion, nationality, and also now of age (at least up to 70, with certain exceptions, some of which will be discontinued by 1982). (4) It is *not* the above-the-table special recruiting and utilization efforts which, *pace* poo-pooing by leaders of some of the recipient groups involved, are not only pressed vigorously, but have been and are being pushed and pressed on a scale that would make a Bear Bryant and Knute Rockne smile a knowing well-done smile. (5) It is *not* even an admission or personnel officer's judgment that, along with sundry other criteria, he or she may take into account an individual applicant's racial, religious, gender, or other characteristics as a "plus"—to use Mr. Justice Powell's crucial *Bakke* term—but only if that applicant can demonstrate the presence of demonstrable explicit or implicit merit in terms of ability and/or genuine promise. For I shall again and again insist that *the* overriding criterion, *the* central consideration, must in the final analysis be present or arguably potential merit. It must thus be merit and ability, not necessarily based exclusively upon past performance, but upon a mature, experienced judgment that merit and ability are in effect in the total picture either by their presence or by their fairly confident predictability. These five aforementioned "nots", which are all aspects of the concept of "affirmative action"—are naturally not an exhaustive enumeration. Yet they are illustrative of common practices that, in my view, do *not* constitute "reverse discrimination"—always provided that they remain appropriately canalized within proper legal and constitutional bounds—for they give life to the basic American right of equality of *opportunity*. One of the major problems, alas, is that militant pro-"reverse discrimination" advocates insist on substituting a requirement of equality of *result* for the requirement of equality of *opportunity*—a requirement based on the dangerous notion of statistical group parity, in which the focal point becomes the *group* rather than the individual.

This brings me to the necessary look at a quintet of what "reverse discrimination" *is*: (1) It *is*, above all, what in the final analysis, the *Bakke, Weber* and *Fullilove* cases fundamentally were all about, namely the setting aside of quotas—be they rigid or quasi-rigid—i.e., the adoption of a *numerus clausus,* on behalf of the admission or recruitment or training or employment or promotion of groups identified and classified by racial, sexual, religious, age or nationality characteristics. For these are characteristics that are, or should be, proscribed on both legal *and* constitutional grounds, because they are *non-sequiturs* on the fronts of individual merit and ability and are, or certainly should be, regarded as being an insult to the dignity and intelligence of the quota recipients. "Our Constitution is color-blind," thundered Mr. Justice John Marshall Harlan in lonely dissent in the famous, or infamous, case of *Plessy v. Ferguson* in 1896, "and neither knows nor tolerates classes among citizens," (163 U.S. 537, at 562). His dissent, which became the guiding star of the Court's unanimous holding in the monumental and seminal 1954 ruling in *Brown v. Board of Education of Topeka, Kansas,* (347 U.S. 483), now prompts us to ask the question whether, as the proponents of "reverse discrimination" urge, the "Constitution must be *color-conscious* in order to be color blind?" But to continue what "reverse discrimination" is, it *is* (2) the slanting of what should be neutral, pertinent, and appropriate threshold and other qualification examinations and/or requirements; double-standards in grading and rating; double-standards in attendance and disciplinary requirements. It *is* (3) the dishonest semanticism of what are called *goals* or *guidelines*, that the latterday bureaucracy has simply pronounced legal and/or constitutional on the alleged grounds that they differ from rigid *quotas*, which admittedly would be presumably illegal and/or unconstitutional. Supported by Mr. Justice Powell's dismissal of them in the *Bakke* decision as a "semantic distinction" which is "beside the point," I submit that this distinction is as unworkable as it is dishonest—in the absence of, to use a favorite Department of Health, Education and Welfare, (and later Health, Education and Human Services), Department of Labor, and O.E.E.O. terms, "good faith" vis-a-vis the far-reaching efforts of affected educational institutions and employers to function under the concept of "goals" or "guidelines."

But while going to enormous lengths to deny any equation of "goals" or "guidelines" with "quotas," the largely Messianic enforcement personnel of the three aforementioned powerful and well-funded agencies of the federal government—personnel that, certainly in the realm of the administration of higher education, often lacks the one-would-think-essential experience and background—in effect *require* quotas while talking "goals" or "guidelines." Indeed, within hours, if not minutes of the *Bakke* decision, for example, Eleanor Holmes Norton, then the agressive head of the O.E.E.O., announced that the Supreme Court holding would make no difference, whatever, in the agency's established policies! Thus, there is extant an eager *presumption* of a lack of a good faith effort against the background-imposition of rigid compliance quotas, based upon frequently irrelevant group statistics, statistics that are demonstrably declared *ultra vires* by Title VII, Sec. 703(j) of the Civil Rights Act of 1964. (4) Reverse discrimination *is* such a statutory provision—one initially challenged and declared unconstitutional by U.S. District Court Judge A. Andrew Hauk, (441 F. Supp. 955) and then upheld by U.S. District Court Judge Daniel J. Snyder, Jr., who was affirmed by the United States Court of Appeals for the Third Circuit—as that mandated under the Public Works Employment Act of 1977. Under that Act, Congress enacted a rigid requirement, adopted on the floor without committee hearings as a result of shrewd strategy by the Congressional Black Caucus, that 10 per cent of all public works contracts designed to stimulate employment go to "minority business enterprises" regardless of the competitiveness of their bid. Known as "M.B.E.'s", they are identified statutorily as private businesses that are at least half-owned by members of a minority group or publicly held businesses in which minority group members control a majority of the stock. For purposes of the Act, "minorities" are defined as "Blacks, Orientals, Indians, Eskimos, Aleuts," and what is termed "the Spanish-speaking." At issue, in what quickly came to be known as the "1977 Ten Per Cent Set-Aside Quota Law," were thousands of construction jobs and billions of dollars worth of Government contracts. But when the U.S. Supreme Court initially had the case before it a few days after it handed down its *Bakke* decision, it ducked the problem on the ground that the award involved had already been consummated and the money expended, the issue thus being moot (438 U.S. 909). However, the Court did then reexamine the matter in 1980 in the seminal case of *Fullilove v. Klutznick* (100 S.Ct. 2758). And reverse discrimination *is* (5) the widely advanced notion, a favorite of officials at the very highest levels of all branches of Administration that, somehow, two wrongs make a right; that the children must pay for the sins of their fathers by self-destructive actions; that of the practice, in the words of Chief Justice Burger's dissenting opinion in the pro-reverse discrimination *Franks* decision in 1976, of "robbing Peter to pay Paul." *(Franks v. Bowman Transportation Co.,* 424 U.S. 747, at 781.)

III.

It is, of course, the latter issue—one I suggested as my fifth illustration of what "reverse discrimination" *is*—that lies at the heart of the matter. To put it simply, but not oversimplifiedly, it is the desire, the perceived duty, the moral imperative, of compensating for the grievous and shameful history of racial and collateral discrimination in America's past. That discrimination is a fact of history which no fair person can deny and the reappearance of which no decent or fair person would sanction, let alone welcome. America's record since the end of World War II, and especially since the *Brown* decision, is a living testament to the far-reaching, indeed exhilarating, ameliorations that have taken place, and are continuing to take place, on the civil rights front. This is a fact of life amply documented and progressively demonstrated, and I need not do so here. (I have tried to do it in my *Freedom and the Court,* due out in its fourth edition in November of 1981) which—ironically, in view of my stance on "reverse discrimination", had encountered difficulties in certain parts of the country as recently as a decade or so ago because of its allegedly excessive liberality on the race issue. I presume it all depends "whose ox is being gored"—to use Al Smith's felicitous phrase—and at which moment in history. Anyone who denies the very real progress *cum* atonement that has taken place, and is continuing to take place, in both the public and the private sector is either a fool, dishonest, or does so for political purposes—and the largest numbers, understandably, fall into that latter category. American society today is absolutely committed to the fullest measure of egalitarianism under our Constitution, mandated in our basic document by the "due process" clause of Amendments Five and Fourteen and the latter's "equal protection of the laws" clause as well as in a plethora of legislation. But 'that Constitution, in the very same Amendments, safeguard *liberty* as well as equality—a somber reminder that rights and privileges are not one-dimensional.

It is on the frontiers of that line between equality and liberty that so much of the "reverse discrimination" controversy, both in its public and private manifestations, has become enbattled. It is here that the insistent, often strident, calls for compensatory, preferential, "reverse discrimination" action are issued—and, more often than not, they issue from a frighteningly profound guilt complex, a guilt complex that has become so pervasive as to brush aside as irrelevant on the altar of atonement even constitutional, let alone legal, barriers—witness, for example, the opinions by Justices Brennan and Blackman in both the *Bakke* and *Weber* rulings. To cite just one or two cases in point: One argument that veritably laces the pro-"reverse discrimination" arguments of the briefs in *Bakke, Weber,* and *Fullilove,* especially those by the American Civil Liberties Union, the Association of American University Professors, Harvard University, Stanford University, the University of Pennsylvania, Columbia University, and the NAACP, among others, is that the injustices of the past justify, indeed demand, a "*temporary* use of affirmative action including class-based hiring preferences and admission goals" in favor of racial minorities. In other words, the record of the past creates the catalyst *cum* mandate for the imposition of *quotas* like the 16 places out of 100 admittedly set aside by the Medical School of the University of California at Davis for the "special" admission of members of certain minority groups. What the school did is entirely straightforward and clear: it *did* establish a racial quota; it *did* practice racial discrimination; it *did* deny admission to a fully qualified white applicant, Allan Bakke, on racial grounds—which as Mr. Justice Stevens's stern opinion for himself and his colleagues Burger, Stewart, and Rehnquist, makes clear, is *ipso facto* forbidden by the plain language of Title VI of the Civil Rights Act of 1964. The University had justified its action on the grounds of redress for past racial discimination (although it had *never* practiced discrimination—and had, and has, never been accused of such until it denied Allan Bakke's admission); on the need for compensatory action; and a commitment to "genuine equal opportunity." In the responsive, apposite words of a widely-distributed statement by the Committee on Academic Nondiscrimination and Integrity:

> Just as no one truly dedicated to civil liberties would contemplate a 'temporary' suspension of, say, the right to counsel or the right to a fair trial as a means of dealing with a crime wave, so no one truly dedicated to equality of opportunity should contemplate a 'temporary' suspension of equal rights of individuals in order to achieve the goal of greater representation. The temporary all too often becomes the permanent. It is not the ultimate ends we proclaim but the temporary means we use which determine the actual future.
>
> (45 *Measure* 1, December 1977.)

In *Weber*, the central issue was a similar type of quota arrangement, although it governed employment rather than education: The Steelworkers and the Kaiser Corporation, under contemporary pressure by government agencies to engage in "affirmative action," had devised a plan that "reserves for black employees 50% of the openings in an in-plant craft training program until the percentage of black craft workers in the plant is commensurate with the percentage of blacks in the local labor force." Both the U.S. District Court and the U.S. Court of Appeals had ruled that the plan clearly violated Title VII, Sec. 703, of the Civil Rights Act of 1964, which *specifically* outlaws discrimination in employment because of "race, color, religion, sex, or national origin" (42 U.S.C.A. § 2000-2 (a), (d), and (j)). But while admitting the presence of the plain statutory proscription, Mr. Justice Brennan in effect sanctioned its violation on the basis of the *spirit* of the law rather than its letter.

In *Fullilove,* the Court—albeit badly split 3:3:3—upheld over "a facial constitutional challenge, a requirement in a congressional spending program that, absent an administrative waiver, 10% of the federal funds granted for local public works projects must be used by the local grantee to procure services or supplies from businesses owned and controlled by members of statutorily identified minority groups." Chief Justice Burger's controlling plurality opinion, joined by Justices White and Powell, found justification in the reach of all spending power which he declared to be "at least as broad as the regulatory powers of Congress," and "properly tailored to cure the effects of prior discrimination."

A related, although somewhat different justification advanced on the altar of redressing past wrongs by temporarily—or perhaps not-so-temporarily?—winking at legal and constitutional barriers, on I prefer to call the "I am not really pregnant, just a little bit," approach to the problem, is illustrated by Ronald Dworkin, Professor of Jurisprudence at Oxford University, in his following 1977 defense of the use of racial critieria in connection with the well-known 1974 Washington Law School "reverse discrimination" case of *De Funis v. Odegaard* (417 U.S. 623).

> Racial criteria are not necessarily the right standards for deciding which applicants should be accepted by law schools for example. But neither are intellectual criteria, nor indeed, any other set of criteria. [*Sic!*] The fairness—and constitutionality—of any admissions program must be tested in the same way. It is justified if it serves a proper policy that respects the right of all members of the community to be treated as equals, but not otherwise . . . We must take care not to use the Equal Protection of the Laws Clause of the Fourteenth Amendment to cheat ourselves of equality. (*Equality and Preferential Treatment*, Princeton University Press, 1977, p. 82.)

Which, of course, is exactly what he in effect counsels—in addition to the inequality of "reverse discrimination." In other words, the desired end justifies the means—no matter what the Constitution may command! We have here another patent illustration of the guilt complex syndrome which, not content with equal justice under law and equality of opportunity, insists upon, in Raoul Berger's characterization, the attainment of "justice at any cost." Yet it represents the gravamen of the concurring opinions in *Bakke* by Justices Brennan, Marshall, and Blackmun; the controlling holding in the *Weber* case via the pen of Mr. Justice Marshall in *Fullilove,* which was joined by his colleagues Brennan and Blackmun.

Along with a good many others who consider themselves *bona fide* civil libertarians and are certifiable champions of civil rights, who decades ago fought the good fight for equal justice and non-discrimination—when fighting it was far more fraught with professional and personal risks than it is now—I confess, however, that I do not have a guilt complex on that issue. Myself a sometime victim of discrimination, of prejudice, and of the *numerus clausus,* i.e. of quotas, I know that two wrongs not one right make; that any so-called "temporary suspension" of constitutional rights, is a cancer upon constitutionalism; that there is no such thing as being a little bit pregnant. Because of our religious persuasion my parental family and I were exiled from, and a number of members of our family were exterminated by, a land where our ancestors had lived for 500 years. As relatively recently as 1952, I was told quite frankly by an administrator at a major Northern University—one of the first proudly to carry the *anti*-Allan Bakke banner twenty-five years later—that I could not be promoted then because "we have already promoted one Jew this year." To which he added, and he was wholly sincere, "no personal offense meant." Happily those times are gone—and I, for one, will not support their return on the altar of siren-like calls for atonement for past wrongs, etched in socio-constitutional rationalizations and manifestations of preferential treatment, compensatory standards, and quotas that are based on criteria and considerations other than those of fundamental merit, of ability, of equality of opportunity, and of equality before the law.

IV.

There is one other matter *cum* issue that must be addressed as a complement to my exhortation of the legal process, the necessity of playing the proverbial judicio-governmental societal game according to its rules. That, of course, is the role of the judiciary in interpreting the Constitution and the laws passed (and executive actions taken) under its constellation. The line between judicial "judging" and "lawmaking" is of course an extremely delicate and vexatious one: what represents "judical activism" to some represents "judicial restraint" to others, and vice versa. All too often an observer's judgment corresponds to the answer to the question "whose ox is gored?" Jurists are human, yet they, unlike laymen, are presumed to be professionally qualified to render objective judgment on the meaning, range, and extent of constitutionally and statutorily sanctioned *or* interdicted governmental authority and exercise of power. To be sure, in Mr. Justice Cardozo's memorable phrase from his seminal *The Nature of the Judicial Process,* (Yale University Press, 1921) "it is not easy to stand aloof" when one deals with so controversial a policy matter as the resort to discrimination as a cure for discrimination, for, as that great jurist and sensitive human being put it so poignantly, "[t]he great tides and currents which engulf the rest of men, do not . . . pass [even] the judges idly by" (p. 168). And they assuredly have not done so—notwithstanding what would appear to be some crystal clear statutory, and some relatively clear constitutional, commands. *Au contraire,* these commands have served jurists as well as legislators and mere citizens as justifications and or rationalizations along the pathways of coming to grips with the issue in settling fashion in either political, or socio-economic, or philosophical, or statutory, or, in the final analysis, judicially constructed terms.

But there *are* demonstrable limits to subjectivity and result orientation, even when these are viewed against the notion of an obligation to heed, as Justice Holmes put it, "the felt necessities of the time" (*The Common Law,* Little, Brown, 1881, p. 1). One of these limits is the ascertainable intent of lawmakers in enacting legislation. *De minimis,* courts have an absolute basic obligation to examine *statutory* language and plain legislative intent as evidenced by the printed record—and the "reverse discrimination" field is no exception. Admittedly, the *constitutional* ground is considerably less clear: for the very verbiage and concept of "equal protection" (and, for that matter, "due process of law") defy finite or categorical definition—regrettably all-too-often depending upon the eye of the beholder or the subject and object of the aforementioned ox-goring. Yet even on constitutional *qua* constitutional grounds it is difficult to deny the verity of Justice Powell's point in his majority opinion in the 1978 *Bakke* case when he noted that: "The guarantee of equal protection cannot mean one thing when applied to one individual and something else when applied to a person of another color. If both are not accorded the same protection, then it is not equal." (438 U.S. 265, at 289-90).

Be that as it may, one who attempts to be a dispassionate commentator need not reach, as in effect the Court customarily tried very hard *not* to reach, the constitutional issue (here the Fourteenth Amendment's equal protection of the laws clause). For if words mean anything, the basic statute involved, namely the 1964 Civil Rights Act's Title VII, would indeed seem to be crystal clear in *proscribing* the kind of racial quotas that the United States District Court and the

United States Circuit Court found to have violated Brian Weber's rights, for example, but which, on appeal, the highest court of the land *upheld* in its 5:2 decision (443 U.S. 193) in 1979. The controlling opinion, written by Mr. Justice Brennan, acknowledged the statutory, the linguistic command; but he and his four supporters found approbative warrant in the law's "spirit" rather than in its letter. For the law's Section 703 (a) makes it unlawful for an employer to classify his employees "in any way which would deprive or tend to deprive any individual of employment opportunities or otherwise adversely effect his status as an employee, because of such individual's race, color, religion, sex, or national origin." And, perhaps even more tellingly, Section 703 (j) provides that the 1964 Act's language is not to be interpreted "to require any employer . . . to grant preferential treatment to any individual or to any group because of the race . . . of such individual or group" to correct a racial imbalance in the employer's work force. Further to buttress historical and factual documentation on statutory grounds that the authors of the Civil Rights Act were demonstrably *opposed* to racial quotas, one need only take a glance at the voluminous, indeed repeated, documentation to that extent in the *Congressional Record* during the debates that led to the passage of the 1964 Civil Rights Act. Thus, the latter's successful Senate floor leader, Senator Hubert Humphrey (D.–Minn.), in responding to concerns voiced by doubting colleagues, vigorously and consistently gave assurance that no racial quotas or racial work force statistics would be employable under the law. In one exchange with his colleague Willis Robertson (D.–Va.), he made the following offer: "If the Senator can find in Title VII . . . any language which provides that an employer will have to hire on the basis of percentage or quota related to color . . . I will start eating the pages one after another, because it is not in there." (110 *Cong. Rec.* 7420).

It is difficult, indeed, it is in fact *impossible,* to argue with the facts of the statute's language or with Congressional intent. Mr. Justice Brennan's opinion attempted to vitiate those facts by (1) seizing upon the allegation that the joint Steelworkers-Kaiser Corporation agreement to hire one black for every white trainee was not required but was *voluntary*; and (2) that, in any event, the program would expire upon reaching statistical workforce-by-race availability-in-the-community parity. One need not embrace the angry and sarcastic language of Mr. Justice Rehnquist's dissenting opinion to support his accurately documented contentions that, as to (1) above, anyone with any knowledge of the course of affirmative action programs knows that they are patently Government-*required*—indeed, inspection from the Office of Federal Contract Compliance Programs had specifically raised the question of Kaiser's compliance; and that, as to (2), provision (j) of Section 703—quoted above—(a) forbids such a program, and (b) the notion that it would prove to be "temporary" is either naive or, as Rehnquist put it, "Houdini"-like. Whatever one's personal views on the underlying issue, whatever one's sympathies, the Rehnquist dissent, as Professor Philip B. Kurland of the University of Chicago School of Law commented, is simply unanswerable in terms of statutory construction and Congressional intent.

To a very considerable degree it was not Mr. Justice Rehnquist's dissent, but that by Mr. Chief Justice Burger, which comes to the heart of the matter if one wishes to abide by the imperatives of the governmental framework under which we function. For he pointed to the salient fact that:

> The Court reaches a result I would be inclined to vote for were I a member of Congress considering a proposed amendment of Title VII. I cannot join the Court's judgement, however, because it is contrary to the explicit language of the statute and arrived at by means wholly incompatible with long-established principles of separation of powers. Under the guise of 'statutory construction,' the Court effectively rewrites Title VII to achieve what it regards as a desirable result. It 'amends' the statute to do precisely what both its sponsors and its opponents agreed the statute was *not* intended to do.
>
> (99 S.Ct. 2721, at 2736.)

There *is no* valid rebuttal to the Chief Justice's admonition—for it assesses accurately the obligations accruing under our system's separation of powers and the attendant roles of the three branches. In brief, and calling a spade a spade, the Court legislated—a function in this instance demonstrably reserved to Congress. The elusive line between "judging" and "legislating" is, to repeat, of course, a monumentally difficult one to draw in a great many instances; it represents *the* basic issue of controversy in the exercise of judicial power. But there is *no* controversy in the present instance: Congress spoke and wrote with indeed uncharacteristic clarity! Nonetheless, a majority of five Supreme Court Justices, given the nature of the public policy issue at hand, would neither listen nor read accurately. The *Weber* decision, in the words of Barbara Lemer, distinguished student of law and psychology, "is a gross and blatant refusal by the Court to enforce the legislative will." (*The Supreme Court Review 1979*, University of Chicago Press, 1980, p. 45.) What the Court in effect did was, as University of Chicago Law professor Edmund W. Kitch put it succinctly, was simply to invalidate the delicate political compromise that led to the Civil Rights [Act] of 1964, namely, that that "law was to enact not a special program of relief and assistance to blacks but a general principle of racial, sexual, religious, and ethnic neutrality." (*Ibid.* p. 3)

A concluding word on the desirability of "reverse discrimination" *per se*. I hope I have demonstrated what I regard as its tenets; what it *is*, and what it is *not*.

Whether or not one agrees with that position, and regardless of how one perceives or reads the inherent statutory and constitutional issues, what of the merits of the proposition of adopting racial, or sexual, or religious, or nationality quotas, or by whatever other noun they may be perfumed? Responding to that *quaere,* I shall call as my star witness upon someone whose credentials on the libertarian front are indisputably impeccable: Justice William O. Douglas. In his 1974 dissenting opinion in *De Funis v. Odegaard,* after finding that Marco De Funis had been rejected by the University of Washington School of Law "solely on account of his race," Douglas lectured at length on that classification, styling it at the outset as introducing "a capricious and irrelevant factor working an invidious discrimination," and insisting that the Constitution and the laws of our land demand that each application for admission must be considered in "a racially neutral way," a phrase he italicized and one, incidentally, quoted with approval by Mr. Justice Powell in *Bakke* "Minorities in our midst who are to serve actively in our public affairs," he went on, "should be chosen on talent and character alone, not on cultural orientation or leanings." (42 LW 4584.) Warmly he had cautioned that there

> is no constitutional right for any race to be preferred . . . A De Funis who is white is entitled to no advantage by reason of that fact nor is he subject to any disability, no matter his race or color. Whatever his race, he had a constitutional right to have his application considered on its individual merits in a racially neutral manner . . . So far as race is concerned, any state sponsored preference of one race over another in that competition is in my view 'invidious' and violative of the Equal Protection Clause. (*Ibid.*)

That exhortation would be eloquently echoed after Douglas's death by Justices Stewart and Stevens's ringing dissenting opinions in *Fullilove*: The former called the 10% set aside law "racist" and an "invidious discrimination by government"; the latter warned that "our statute books will once again have to contain laws that reflect the odious practice of delineating the qualities that make one person a Negro and make another white, and suggested sarcastically that now our government must devise its version of the Nazi Nurnberg laws that defined who was and who was not a Jew. (48 LW 4979, at 5002-5007.)

Justice Douglas—who in his last book, wrote that, "Racial quotas—no matter how well-intentioned—are a wholly un-American practice, quite inconsistent with equal protection—had concluded his *De Funis* dissent on a note that, for me, hits the essence of the entire issue: "The Equal Protection Clause," he insisted commands the elimination of racial barriers, not their creation in order to satisfy our theory as to how society ought to be organized. The purpose of the University of Washington cannot be to produce Black lawyers for Blacks, Polish lawyers for Poles, Jewish lawyers for Jews, Irish lawyers for the Irish. It should be to produce good lawyers for Americans . . .

(42 LW 4584, at 4586)

That, I submit in all humility, is the *sine qua non* of the matter. It is my fervent hope, though very far from a confident expectation—especially in view of the unsatisfactory, multi-faceted, evasion-inviting response given by the Court in *Bakke* and the high tribunal's patent violation of the language and intent of Title VII in *Weber*—that we will still, at this late hour, resolve to heed the now deceased Justice's admonition and substitute for "lawyers" whatever educational, occupational, or professional noun may be appropriate in given circumstances in the justly egalitatian strivings of all Americans, regardless of race, sex, creed, nationality, or religion, for a dignified, happy, prosperous, and free life, blessed by a resolute commitment to and acquiescence in equal justice under law—which is as the cement of society.